WATERSTONE'S

17/04/98 10:36   J   17   10110
  1 @ 14.95 0907771602   £   14.95*
            CORFU INCIDENT.

TOTAL   £   14.95
TENDER CASH   £   20.00
CHANGE   £   5.05

8 ROYAL AVE, BELFAST, BT1 1DA
TEL: 01232 247355 VAT NO: 710 631 184

THE CORFU INCIDENT

The
Corfu
Incident

Eric Leggett

Liskeard
Maritime Books

First Published in Great Britain 1974 by
SEELEY SERVICE & CO. LTD.,
196 Shaftesbury Avenue,
London WC2 8JL

This Edition Published by
MARITIME BOOKS,
Liskeard,
Cornwall PL14 4EL

01579 343663

Copyright © 1974 by Eric Leggett

ISBN 0 907771 60 2

Made & Printed in Great Britain by
Antony Rowe Ltd.,
Chippenham,
Wiltshire SN14 6LH

CONTENTS

1 The Warning Shots *1*
2 Murder in the Channel *19*
3 The End of the Affair *121*
Epilogue *156*

APPENDICES

I The Men who Died *157*
II Captain Selby's Report *159*
III Case Histories of the Four Ships *163*
IV The *Saumarez* and the *Scharnhorst* *175*
V A Corfiot eye-witness *178*

AUTHOR'S NOTE

I am deeply grateful to the many people who have given me their assistance during the research and preparation of this book. But my deepest debt of gratitude is to those survivors of H.M.S. *Saumarez* and H.M.S. *Volage* who drew back the comforting curtain of time and re-lived incidents, many of them painful in the extreme, which for a quarter of a century they had tried to forget. In that respect this book is as much theirs as it is mine.

ERIC LEGGETT
1974

1

The Warning Shots

THE pearly, luminous haze which often comes with dawn in the Mediterranean lifted as the two British warships slipped past the last of the small Ionian Islands and headed for the channel which divides the island of Corfu from the coast of Albania. As the two ships turned to starboard to enter the channel the look-outs and officers of the watch studied the Albanian coast. It was an impressive sight—gaunt, granite-grey, sheer-faced cliffs rearing straight out of the sea as if some mighty under-water hand had heaved them bodily towards the sky.

The date was 15 May, 1946, and for the men aboard the two ships there seemed nothing special in that; just another day at sea in the peace-time Mediterranean Fleet; polishing the bright-work, washing the upper deck paintwork, your tot of rum at mid-day and if you're lucky the ships would stop in the dog watches and the bosun's mates would pipe 'Hands over the side to bathe'. And, at the signal, the ships' engines would stop and hundreds of men would leap over the ships' sides into their own vast, private swimming pool—the Mediterranean.

But, to the captains and navigating officers of the two ships, the cruisers H.M.S. *Orion* and H.M.S. *Superb*, there was something which made this sea passage a little out of the ordinary. During the war which had just ended the Germans had laid two huge minefields to guard the channel. For the convenience of their own shipping they had maintained throughout the war years a safe corridor one mile wide through the mine barrage. When the tide of war turned against the Germans and they retreated northwards, the Allies took over the area and British minesweepers carried out what is known as a check-sweep. No mines were found in the corridor and it was declared safe for all shipping. The *Orion* and the *Superb* were the first British warships to use the mine-free corridor since the end of the war. The passage, from north to south, would require careful navigation, but there was certainly nothing in the operation to tax the professional skills and experience of the officers on the bridges of the two ships.

Almost simultaneously the bosun's mates on each ship went to their Tannoy broadcasters and the shrill wailing of the bosuns' pipes pierced the swish of the bow waves and the whine of the light breeze in the signal halyards.

'Call the hands. Call the hands. Wakey wakey, rise and shine.' The look-outs on duty for the morning watch enjoyed that slightly vindictive feeling of 'Yes, get out of those hammocks you lazy . . . we've been up here since four o'clock.'

As the seamen emerged on to the upper deck and began, bare-foot, to scrub the quarter deck and the port and starboard waists with their long-handled scrubbers, officers on the two bridges were studying charts on which the mineswept corridor was marked. *Orion*, wearing the flag of Rear-Admiral H. R. G. Kinahan, was in the lead. The *Superb* followed directly in her wake at a steady ten knots.

The two ships were completely different in outline and background. The *Orion*, built in 1932, had been through a busy war in the Mediterranean, her actions including Matapan —where the Italian Fleet was routed—and the invasion beaches of Anzio. The *Superb* was a brand new vessel—the first of the *Tiger* class—and she had never fired a shot in anger. The original crew which commissioned her at the yard of her builders, Swan Hunter of Wallsend-on-Tyne, were actually on their final leave before sailing her out to the war against Japan when the atom bombs on Hiroshima and Nagasaki so abruptly ended the war in the Far East. The *Superb* never did go to the Far East and eventually appeared in the Mediterranean. Her masts were festooned with all the latest and most sophisticated radar and direction-finding aerials, making her one of the most easily recognizable warships in the world. This point was, in the space of about an hour, to assume critical significance.

As the members of *Orion's* crew not on watch sat at breakfast an officer came on the Tannoy and told them that the country on the port side was Albania and gave them a potted version of the country's recent history. And a turbulent background it had been. After centuries of foreign domination, the Albanians had finally kicked out the last of their tormentors, the Germans, and the Communists had seized power.

Under Europe's newest dictator, Enver Hoxha, the present régime had silenced, by death or disgrace, all opposition. Tito's Yugoslavia and Stalin's Russia were now the country's only friends. Barred frontiers and armed guards kept the world out and the Albanian people in. It was a brooding, secretive enigma of a country. To its geographical remoteness it had now added the isolation of its new-found ideology. A quarter of a century later Albania remains as secretive and enigmatic as ever it was.

Up on the bridge of the *Orion* the order was given for the two cruisers to make the right-hand turn of the dog-leg route through the mine-free corridor. Because the coastline of Corfu, with its gradually shelving shores and submerged rocks made it dangerous for shipping, the swept corridor sometimes hugged the Albanian shore. It was at one of these points in the route, off the Albanian port of Saranada, that the turn to starboard had to be made. At that moment the two cruisers were less than a mile from Albanian territory. The captains, officers of the watch and look-outs scanned the towering coastline. The warmth of the early morning sun had melted the mists which since dawn had flirted with the mountain peaks, now hiding, now revealing, as though to add coquetry to an already mysterious land. Occasional long, thin scars down the mountain sides were identified as tracks so steep that only donkeys or goats could use them. They saw no one, no movement, nothing. The port of Corfu now lay almost dead ahead, through the narrowest part of the channel, where Albania and Corfu Island are a mere three miles apart. In these narrows the border between Albania and Greek territory runs down the centre of the channel, leaving one and a half miles of the sea as Greek territorial waters and the other one and a half miles as belonging to Albania. Up forward, the forecastle parties aboard the two ships were preparing to anchor in the vast, semi-circular harbour of Corfu. They were due there in about an hour, at 9.30 a.m.

Suddenly this idyllic scene was shattered by an incident which was to lead directly, and only five months hence, to the blowing up of two other British warships, the destroyers *Saumarez* and *Volage*, and the deaths of forty-four sailors in circumstances which amounted to deliberate, controlled, cold-blooded murder by the Albanians.

On that sunny May morning a seaman working on the quarter deck of the *Superb* saw a belch of white smoke on the hill-side, which was by now receding astern of the two ships. Then he heard a bang. 'Rather like a car back-firing,' he thought. To his astonishment, a reaction subsequently to be shared by the whole of Britain, a water-spout shot up about 200 yards astern of the *Superb*. Someone was actually firing on the British Navy from the Albanian shore!

Less than a minute later another water-spout appeared in the wake of the *Superb*. Members of the ships' companies crowded the guard rails and peered towards the shore batteries. Mystification was on every face. On the bridge of *Orion*, Rear-Admiral Kinahan was equally puzzled. The shots could hardly be construed as a warning to stand farther off the Albanian coast, because they had fallen astern of the two ships. He had received no warning signal from the shore. Both ships were flying the big white ensigns they had just hoisted ready for entering Corfu harbour, replacing the smaller ensigns flown at sea. They should have been clearly seen from the gun positions by anyone using binoculars. In any case, if the officer commanding the battery could not recognize two well-known ships of the Royal Navy, each with a distinctive shape, then he was either incompetent or mad, or both. And the sooner out of his range, the better. Admiral Kinahan gave the order for both ships to increase speed towards Corfu.

But the firing continued. Something like twelve shots from what were judged to be four-inch calibre guns were fired at the ships. As the cruisers rapidly widened the range, the shore gunners became more inaccurate and the shells dropped farther and farther astern of the ships.

In Corfu harbour Admiral Kinahan immediately reported the incident to his Commander-in-Chief, Admiral Sir Algernon Willis.

The British public had to wait eight days before the newspapers published reports of this insult to national pride. The reaction was just as it had been in the Mediterranean Fleet— something to chuckle about, rather than rage over. Really, these Albanians are asking for a punch on the nose if they carry on like this!

The reason for the Government's suppression of news of the incident has never been explained. But it almost certainly lies in the fact that the incident had occurred at a most unfortunate time. The Labour Government of Clement Attlee, devoted as it was to the principle of nations having the freedom to run their own affairs, was sympathetic towards Albania and was prepared to consider exchanging ambassadors. The Government was no doubt pleased of a few days of silence to sort out the diplomatic muddle.

The outcome was that the exchange of ambassadors was called off and the inevitable exchange of diplomatic Notes began. The British Government protested about the outrageous incident, demanded an apology and the punishment of the person responsible for inflicting this indignity.*

The Albanians replied that it had all been a mistake. The

* Far from punishing the commander of the battery, one Captain Backa, the Albanians subsequently promoted him.

5

commander of the shore battery signalled the ships but they continued to head straight into Saranda Bay. (It was essential for the ships to do this to keep within the swept corridor. The dog-leg turn to starboard previously mentioned eventually took the ships away from Saranda.)

The Note gave a different version of the hoisting of the ensigns aboard the two cruisers. Admiral Kinahan's report to Admiral Willis made it clear that ensigns, either the smaller ones flown during the sea passage, or the larger ones hoisted ready for entering Corfu harbour, were flown by the two cruisers at all times. The Albanian Note said the battery commander ordered his guns to cease firing when the ships hoisted their ensigns. The incident was regretted and it was hoped there would be no lasting damage to relations with Britain.

That Note might well have ended the exchange between Britain and Albania there and then, but for one word in it. Albania referred to the presence of the British ships in her territorial waters as an 'intrusion'. The British Government's reaction to the use of this word was one of astonishment and anger. The reply was a finger-wagging lecture on international law and the status of international waterways. The crux of Britain's argument, and it was fully supported by law and practice, was that the Corfu Channel was an international sea highway and, as such, entitled to be used by ships of any nation on innocent passage through it.

The fact that ships doing so would pass close to Albania's coast was of no significance because, in a channel only three miles across at its narrowest point, neither nation could claim the whole of the three miles as its own territorial waters.

Albania could not, the British Government declared, decide which ships could use the channel and which could not. Further exchanges between the two countries proved that, far from accepting this verbal wigging from the strongest maritime nation in the Mediterranean, tiny, backward, isolated Albania was prepared to take defiance to the point of re-writing international law to her own benefit.

She alleged that Greek ships, including warships, had frequently approached close to the Albanian shore in the channel[*] In future, she declared, all foreign warships and merchant vessels would have to get permission from Albania before sailing within three miles of her coast through the channel. This demand, if accepted, would have closed the Corfu Channel to all ships which had not been granted Albania's permission.

Britain's reply was, of course, one of complete non-acceptance. In Whitehall there was growing impatience with a country which just would not accept facts as they always had been and as they must remain. Albania's attitude was just not civilized. If she were going to grow up to live within a community of nations, albeit with a different political system, she would just have to learn right from wrong. The thought that Albania might be prepared to resort to something stronger than words, or four-inch shells, to back up her demands occurred to no one. If anyone had been foolish enough to venture such a thought, it would certainly have been dismissed as preposterous nonsense.

And to show that she, too, could get tough, and had more to get tough with, Britain warned Albania that the Navy would fire back if the coastal batteries ever again fired on British warships. The Albanian Government could have been in no doubt as to the outcome of such an event. The Royal Navy ended the war with nearly 3,000 warships. While many of these had gone out of commission, it remained a mighty force and some of the most powerful vessels were with the Mediterranean Fleet. If the Fleet had turned only half its fire power on the shore batteries, they would have been obliterated in minutes.

Unknown to the British public, there now began the slow, inexorable escalation of events which was to lead to the disaster of 22 October. This may best be shown by quoting four

* Albania and Greece were, at this time, disputing some border territories. There is some evidence to believe that Albania feared an invasion of her territory by Greece.

significant messages that passed between the Admiralty and Admiral Willis, C-in-C Mediterranean Fleet. The first message, transmitted from London on 1 August, said:

> H.M. Ambassador has now been instructed to present a Note to the Albanian Government giving reasons why H.M. Government do not consider the reply of the Albanian Government to be satisfactory, and concluding with the words: 'Furthermore the Albanian Government should take note that should the Albanian coastal batteries in the future open fire on any of H.M. vessels passing through the Corfu Channel, fire will be returned.' In the meantime you should continue to refrain from using the Channel.

That telegram, submitted as a certified true copy, was part of Britain's evidence against Albania when the case of the two mined destroyers went before the International Court at The Hague. Britain refused to reveal to the Court the exact wording of the following three messages, claiming that it was necessary to safeguard naval cyphers. The wording as submitted to the Court was said to be an accurate paraphrase of the texts.

Message number two in the series was sent by the Admiralty on 10 August. It told Admiral Willis:

> Albanians have now received the Note. North Corfu strait may now be used by ships of your fleet, but only when essential and with armament in fore and aft position. If coastal guns fire at ships passing through the strait, ships should fire back.

Telegram number three in the series was sent from the Admiralty to Admiral Willis on 21 September. It disclosed a new development in the affair, the possibility of re-opening diplomatic relations with Albania. But more significantly, as time was to show, it contained a phrase so embarrassing to the British Government that the person who drafted the message must, in retrospect, have wished a sudden attack of cramp had

8

. .

given him time to pause and think again. In this telegram the phrase is printed in italics:

> Establishment of diplomatic relations with Albania is under consideration by H.M. Government, *who wish to know whether the Albanians have learned to behave themselves.* Information is requested whether any ships under your command have passed through the North Strait since August and, if not, whether you intend them to do so shortly.

Of course this message was never intended to be known to anyone outside the Admiralty and the C-in-C. High officials of the Civil Service and senior officers of the three Services frequently do express themselves in down to earth terms (and why not?) safe in the knowledge that Acts designed to maintain Government secrets will usually protect them throughout their lifetime.

But these telegrams were eventually required for presentation before the highest court of justice in the world. When this particular phrase was revealed at The Hague, the Albanian Government's legal representatives seized upon it with the delight of a man who has been losing a fight and then is suddenly presented with the chance to grab his enemy's own stick and beat him about the head with it.

Albania's Chief Advocate was M Pierre Cot, a wily and devious French lawyer who fought for Albania's case with a ferocity which frequently startled the witnesses he was cross-examining. Waving his copy of the telegram aloft he declared that it proved what Albania had been saying since Britain first refused diplomatic recognition of her Communist Government, that the United Kingdom's attitude towards Albania was in the worst tradition of a colonial power dealing with a minor vassal. At the best interpretation it smacked of a heavy-handed father keeping a small child in his place. At the worst it was arrogant, bullying, 'Big Brother' tactics of the most reprehensible kind.

Viewed with the benefit of twenty-five years' hindsight, it is difficult to deny that the Albanian's case, so forcefully expressed by M Cot, had a considerable element of truth. The British Government *did* adopt an excessively paternalistic attitude towards the Albanians. It *did*, by the peevish tone of its Notes, correct though they were in international law and common practice, give the impression of dealing with a somewhat tiresome little boy newly come into the neighbourhood who simply did not know his table manners.

History may say that Albania had already decided that, if its resolve not to knuckle down to Big Brother Britain meant the two countries were on collision course, so be it. One is, however, entitled to take the view that, whatever the strength of Albania's feelings at the time, her will to resist Britain's interference was fortified beyond all measure by the British Government's inability to take her seriously.

And so we arrive at the fourth and final telegram between the Admiralty and Admiral Willis. It will be recalled that the third telegram to the Admiral merely asked whether any ships under his command had passed through the Corfu Channel since August 'and, if not, whether you intend them to do so shortly'.

Why the Admiralty did not *instruct* Admiral Willis to send ships through the Corfu Channel when their intention clearly was that he should do so has never been made clear. It is now of academic interest. Admiral Willis got the Admiralty message in more ways than one, as his reply to the Admiralty, sent the following day, clearly shows:

> They have not done so yet, but my intention is that Admiral Kinahan, flying his flag in *H.M.S. Mauritius*, with *H.M.S. Leander* and two destroyers, should do so when they depart from Corfu on 22 October.

Having sent off his telegram, Admiral Willis instructed his staff officers to change the arranged programmes for the four ships. On 22 October, instead of turning south on leaving Corfu and heading by the most direct route, to Argostoli on the Greek island of Cephalonia, they would turn north to sail deliberately and provocatively through the Corfu Channel to see 'whether the Albanians have learned to behave themselves'.

And so the scene was set, the cast chosen, the location in no doubt. And, like many a piece of ancient Greek history played out on those very seas, it would end in tragedy.

At this point it is necessary to analyse one of the great paradoxes of post-war history. It can be expressed in one sentence: Why did Albania, an impoverished, battered, backward, isolated country, only a fifth of the size of England, decide to defy a nation which had just emerged victorious from the Second World War, and to provoke and finally take on, the whole might of the then considerable British Navy?

The answer to that question lies buried in the proud and turbulent history of the Albanian people. In that sense the story of the Corfu Incident begins not on 22 October, 1946, not even in May of that year when the shots fired from the Albanian coast foreshadowed the disaster to come.

Its origins lie in the struggle of the Albanian people down the centuries to throw off one oppressor after another and finally, in October, 1944, having defeated their last tormentors, the Germans, to achieve their own independence, albeit a Communist one. For it is only by understanding these centuries of suffering and humiliation that we can hope to understand the fierce national pride which inevitably led Albania to her confrontation with Britain.

Certainly from a strict historical point of view, it was no new experience for Albania to face up to the might of a powerful Empire. For more than 2,000 years the country had been marched over by the armies of its foreign oppressors. It began with the Romans. Albania was then successively occupied by the Goths, the Serbs, the Bulgars, the Greeks, the Normans. After a second period of Serbian rule around 1400 the country split into small areas each occupied by one tribe. This fragmentation was to have the most catastrophic results. It provided easy pickings for the next invader, the one which was to have an influence seen today in buildings, religion, and the way of life of the Moslem East—the Turks.

Skanderbeg, to this day Albania's most famous soldier and her national hero, fought for twenty years to rally the tribal chiefs and kept the might of the Ottoman Empire at bay. When he was killed Albania began the dark night, 500 years long, of Turkish occupation. It was, as history has shown most occupations to be, cruel and rapacious. And the Turks, through centuries of experience, brought a new meaning to the words cruelty and rapacity. The Moslem religion was imposed with a ferocity of purpose which few could survive in the areas under the direction domination of the Turks.*

The Moslem laws of segregation of the sexes put the Albanian women behind the veils of the East. To the country as a whole these veils must have seemed symbolic of a final curtain being drawn across their centuries of history. Turkish war lords ruled their individual domains living in the splendour of vast palaces, harems, silken robes and jewels, while the peasants scratched for a living in a harsh country where 80 per cent of the acreage was, and still is, a wasteland of razor-back mountains, swamps and dried-up river beds. The slightest offence by the peasant population brought the most terrible retribution. A slow death by being impaled like a carcase of meat on a hook was one of the less esoteric forms of execution.

And so Albania lived for 500 terrible years, cut off from its historic and geographic links with Europe, the people forbidden to speak their own language, their monuments smashed, their culture stamped into the ground.

Resistance occasionally flared, but each pathetic attempt to throw off the yoke of the Turkish Empire was defeated not so much by the cruel, repressive methods of the Turks, but by that in-built characteristic of the Faith two-thirds of the Albanians had been forced to accept, the fatalism of the Moslem creed.

'We peasants are doomed to work and to suffer,' they would say. 'Has it not always been so? The Turks are destined to

* In the wild, virtually impregnable country, and in the area close to the Greek border, the Roman Catholic faith and the Orthodox religion remained alive.

oppress us and grow rich and powerful. It has always been that way; it always will be. It is Fate. It is no use fighting against it. Death will come quick enough.'

But, as even the darkest night must end, so did the grip of the Turkish Empire on Albania begin to weaken. In the late ninetenth century young men of courage formed the Albanian League, an organization sworn to fight for the country's freedom from the Turks. Uprisings between 1909 and 1912 led to the proclamation of independence and, in July, 1913, the European powers accepted Albania's independence.

This freedom was short-lived. With the outbreak of the First World War in 1914, French, Italian and Serbian troops occupied various regions of the country by declaring it a protectorate, foreshadowing the moment when history would repeat itself thirty years later. When, after bitter wrangling, Italy withdrew in 1920, Albania was recognized as an independent state and was governed as a constitutional republic.

But Fate had not yet finished with Albania. Only eight years later the country was plunged into darkness once again when Achmed Zogu, a tribal chief with little intellect but unbounding ambition, decided that being President of Albania did not satisfy his grandiose ambitions and declared himself King.

For the Albanians the régime of King Zog, as he became known, must have recalled the horrors of the hated Turks. Zog gave immense power to the feudal landlords, just as the Turks had claimed similar powers for themselves.

A graphic insight into this new oppression is given by Dymphna Cusack, one of the few Western observers allowed into Albania since the Communists came to power.*

She writes of meeting an old peasant, on the snow-covered plateau of Korca, who talked of the rule of one of these feudal landlords, Maliq Bey:

Illyria Reborn, Heinemann, 1966. Miss Cusack made a six-month tour of the country in 1964. Her book deals sympathetically with Albania's history and lyrically with its attempts to rebuild and modernize the country. Strangely, it makes no mention of The Corfu Incident and the fact that Albania then stood, and still stands, guilty of the deaths of forty-four British sailors.

'Until the liberation the whole plateau belonged entirely to the beys,' he told us. 'In the old days this village was surrounded by a large wall. Inside the wall the bey owned everything. No peasant could build even a rough hut outside the walls unless he agreed that it should belong to the bey. Any peasant putting up a hut had to put his thumb-mark to paper. In those days hardly any of us could write our names. (He pointed to a vast plain.) If you look at an old map you'll see that all this was called the Marshes of Maliq. Not only were we poor but in winter the villages used to be flooded when the lake overflowed, and in the summer they were infested with malarial mosquitoes.

'Maliq Bey owned the whole of the area of Maliq and he sold various rights for fishing and game hunting. He would lend money to us peasants at interest of 20 per cent, so that we never had a chance of getting out of debt. That's how I lived and my father lived and my grand-father lived before him.'

Dymphna Cusack also records the director of an agricultural co-operative telling her:

'During Zogu's time many of the peasants from this region emigrated because they couldn't stand Maliq Bey's oppression any more. In addition to having to pay him a third of what the land produced, every Saturday we had to take him gifts of eggs, chickens and honey, though we never ate anything but corn bread and kos (yogurt) ourselves. As well as all that we had the national taxes, including a poll tax.

'There was only one school for every four or five villages, and only children of the rich peasants could go to it. In spite of that, we peasants had to pay a school tax. Maliq Bey and the other three lesser beys in the area had a contract between them which set out "Those are your peasants those are mine," and no peasant who got into trouble with his bey had any hope of living in the district. They did not even stop short of murder; for instance, the son of Maliq Bey was a killer; he killed three people during the Zogu régime, including a doctor in Korca whom he killed with a knife. Absolutely nothing was done by the Government in Tirana or the local police to bring him to justice. During the war they collaborated with the Germans.'

It is well to pause for a moment to reflect that tyranny of this kind was happening, not in medieval times, but in a European country in the 1930's.

From the moment he seized power Zog, as the Turks before him, did nothing to curb the curse of Albania—the Vendetta, the code which honour demanded should take a life for a life. After all, how much easier to keep the peasants under control if they were for ever fighting and feuding among themselves.

The Vendetta was originally born out of poverty and quarrels over sheep and grazing rights. It became invested down the centuries with the sanctity of a crusade. The peasants had so little; let no man try to take away his honour, unless he be prepared to risk his own life! Blood for blood; that was the law. It has been recorded that whole families of sons were killed, one after the other, as they tried to avenge the death of a father.

Feuds were passed on from generation to generation. Men were often prisoners in their own homes for five, ten, even fifteen years; they knew that if they ventured outside 'Their Enemy', the words which haunted their lives, would surely kill them.

If a husband were killed during his wife's pregnancy, she would pray for a son. And, if she were so blessed, his duty to avenge his father's death was the first word he heard on his mother's knee.

It is part of the enigma which was, and still is, Albania that a nation which has suffered so much from oppressors of the outside world should torture itself even further with self-inflicted wounds. Life has always been held cheap in Albania.

The relatives of the men who died aboard *Saumarez* and *Volage*, and the men who survived, are entitled to the view that the lives of outsiders are reckoned cheaper still.

Towards the end of the 1920's two events, which no one could possibly recognize as having a dual significance, took place. The first was that King Zog, living the life of a 'little Sultan' on money filched from the State Treasury, tried to secure his comfortable and luxurious future by signing a defensive alliance with the Fascist dictatorship of Mussolini's Italy.

The second was when a young student called Enver Hoxha, sickened by his country's past and dismayed by its apparent future as a lackey of a Fascist Government, emigrated to Paris and there studied, and later preached, pure Marxist-Leninist Communism.

For Zog, his decision led directly into exile. The Italians gradually increased their hold on the country and, in 1939, Mussolini's troops invaded. Zog fled, never to return.

For Enver Hoxha, his decision led directly to the dictatorship of his country, a position he still holds today, and the confrontation with Britain over the Corfu incident.

After his studies in Paris Hoxha returned to Albania and ran a tobacconist's shop in Tirana. It was in fact the Communist Party headquarters for the country. There, until the invasion of his country in 1939, he built cadres of dedicated Communists.

When war broke out and the Germans swept into the country, he took to the mountains and joined the Partisans. He proved himself to be as skilful with weapons as he was with words. When the Germans were finally driven from Albania he had the rank of Colonel-General and was the obvious choice to lead the revolution the Communists were already planning. He took over power in October, 1944, and, a month later, proclaimed the 'first democratic government of Albania'.

Hoxha, at the head of this provisional Government, at once descended on his opponents, or suspected opponents, with a ruthlessness which must have delighted his idol, Stalin himself. Old friends were among those driven from public office, or from positions of power in industry, the civil service, the courts. For some the word 'eliminated' meant just that.

Hoxha then set about the daunting task of rebuilding the country with methods of pure Communism which must have brought further approving nods from Stalin and from Hoxha's boyhood hero, Marshal Tito, dictator of the neighbouring Communist Yugoslavia.

Albania's pitifully few factories were nationalized.* Agreements with foreign countries, solemnly made, were cancelled overnight. The middle classes and 'war profiteers'—Hoxha branded them as one and the same—were taxed into the ground.

By late 1945, through a policy of icy ruthlessness against friends and enemies alike, at home and abroad, this thick-set, baby-faced man, still only thirty-eight, was able to demand elections for a permanent form of Government for Albania, and to be confident of the outcome. He was not disappointed.

In December, 1945, Hoxha's Party received 93 per cent of the votes. The following month Colonel-General Enver Hoxha, resplendent in one of the elaborate uniforms he loved to wear, stood before the Constituent Assembly and declared Albania a Popular Republic.

The British Government was furious. Displaying that paternalism towards small nations which came so easy when 'half the map was red', Britain had, quoting her support of Albania through the war as the right, demanded that foreign observers should administer the December elections to make sure that they were free. The order outraged Hoxha. He rejected it as an 'insult' and, in speeches up and down the country, ranted against the Imperialists who could not understand that Albania had at last won her freedom after 2,000 years and was determined to keep it.

In the same mood he refused America's offer of Marshall

---

* Albania's industry at that time comprised a cement factory, a brewery, some tobacco factories, a few small brick and tile works and several flour mills.

Aid, preferring to drive his country into the twentieth century by its own efforts, rather than by 'Wall Street hand-outs with their strings attached'. Rarely had a hand which fed so lavishly been bitten so fiercely.

But Hoxha's anger was to be expressed in more than words. He began the wholesale expulsion of all foreigners of Western Governments. With little ceremony and even less thanks, members of the British military mission, many of whom had fought side by side with Hoxha's partisans, and supplied them with arms, food and money, were kicked out. Civilians ready to administer further financial aid to Albania, even civilians of the War Graves Commission, all were ordered to leave.

Angered, and bewildered, by this ingratitude, both the British and American Governments refused to recognize Hoxha's Communist government. That Britain at least firmly believed Albania's peevish behaviour would not last for long will be shown by later events.

In Government circles the Albanians' attitude was likened to that of a small boy sticking his tongue out at his big brother —give him time and he will learn manners. Rarely has one Government so seriously miscalculated the attitudes and reactions of another.

Hoxha, now virtually cut off from the Western Powers, moved even closer to the two men who had always been his idols, Tito and Stalin. The Iron Curtain came down around Albania even before Winston Churchill popularized the phrase later that year.

Unless the British Government, even at this late stage, could accept Hoxha's sincerity when he declared that Albania was prepared to defend her borders by land or sea, The Corfu Incident, or something like it, was inevitable.

The British Government did not believe Hoxha. They still did not believe him when, four months later, the *Superb* and the *Orion* were fired on by the Albanian shore batteries.

Inevitability now had to run its fatal course.

2

Murder in the Channel

T HOUSANDS of Maltese men and women with dark-haired, dark-eyed children clutching their hands, stood on the massive terraced walls of Grand Harbour, Valletta, as the Mediterranean Fleet of the Royal Navy sailed for its goodwill cruise of the Eastern Mediterranean.

On that day in the early autumn of 1946, Malta still showed the gaping wounds from the brutal battering it had received from German bombers in 2,000 air raids. Everywhere the stonemasons were cutting up the local stone, so soft it can be sliced with cross-cut saws, to patch and rebuild the shattered homes, churches and ancient castles.

In the harbour masts, and occasionally the tip of a funnel thrusting above the surface of the water, showed how many ships, sunk by those same bombers, remained to be lifted from the sea-bed. But as the warships threaded their way through the sunken ships and headed out to sea, every person watching the proud sight must have said to himself: 'Everything is going to be all right now, just like it always was; we'll soon be back to our normal way of life; the Navy is cruising again.'

The sight of a Mediterranean Fleet steaming out of Grand Harbour, exchanging salutes with Fort Ricasoli guarding the entrance, was a symbol for everyone, the Maltese as well as crews aboard the warships, that war was over and peace was here at last.

Together the Fleet travelled to the Bay of Nauplia in

Greece. From Nauplia the Fleet split up into various units, each to carry out individual programmes of goodwill visits to various ports, and simulated exercises and 'war games' which everyone from captains down to boy seamen sooner or later found childish and boring. And so it was that, on 17 October, *Mauritius* and *Leander*, *Saumarez* and *Volage*, sailed into the port of Corfu. For four days their crews enjoyed their 'runs ashore', as shore leave is known.

At first glance it appeared that few of the traditional pleasures of the sailor were available in Corfu at that time. The town itself seemed, as did many places in the Mediterranean, to be shrugging the effects of war from its shoulders. Although the battles of the Mediterranean had flowed round the seas off Corfu without harming her, the deprivations of war were still in evidence. Food was in short supply. The streets, often just dirt tracks in the old part of the town, had a squalid, unkempt air. The ancient courtyards, which today's tourists photograph bright with geranium and pelargonium, were dark and dusty. Even the people of Corfu, normally gay and vivacious by nature, seemed dull and morose, as though they were still not fully awakened from the years of war.

The sailors spent their time in the few bars that were open or buying the local hand-made lace for their wives, sweethearts or mothers, or sending home parcels of the locally grown figs and currants, for strict rationing was still in force in Britain.

Very few of the sailors managed to work up any interest in the history of Corfu, with the exception of a number of ex-public schoolboys who were either going back to university on demobilization, or who were hoping to transfer to the regular Royal Navy and go to Dartmouth to study for a commission.

Corfu's history stretches back to mythical times. It was here that Odysseus was shipwrecked, a fate which was tempered by his being held prisoner for seven years by Nausicaa, the beautiful daughter of King Alcinous. The Romans conquered Corfu in 229 B.C. and it remained part of the Roman Empire until it was handed over to the Turks in A.D. 773. Towards the end of the fourteenth century, the Venetians took over and their influence lasted until 1797 and can still be seen in many of the main buildings in the town of Corfu, particularly in the Church of St Spyridon and in the town's fortresses.

The French, who took the island during the Napoleonic wars, left their influence in The Liston, a row of elegant arcades reminiscent of the Rue de Rivoli in Paris. After the defeat of Napoleon, Britain ruled Corfu for half a century, and made a unique contribution by introducing cricket to the island. It is still played there. Another and more eminent association with Britain is to be found in a palace two miles outside Corfu town. At this palace, the summer residence of the Greek Royal Family (and bearing the most unpalatial name of *Mon Repos*) was born a young Greek prince who, in 1946, was serving in the Royal Navy as Lieut Philip Mountbatten.

But for the active service sailors, the men who had joined the Navy before the war and had fought through it, the veneer of toughness which is acquired by service effectively shielded them from any encroachment of culture. That was for the youngsters who had not yet 'got their knees brown'.*

---

* The Mediterranean Fleet at that time was of particularly strange composition. It has been estimated that upwards of three-quarters of the men were youngsters who had joined up just before the war ended as 'Hostilities Only' ratings and were awaiting demobilization. They were in their late teens or early twenties. The remaining quarter of the Fleet personnel were long-service men who had joined the Navy before the war and were still serving out their time. The slow switch-over to a smaller peace-time Navy was causing great difficulties and the demobilization system certainly did not work smoothly. There were, for instance, surpluses of men in some trades (writers and stewards), who were therefore released quickly. The rate of release of men in some trades (particularly the seaman branch) was deliberately slowed down. Some men who volunteered for 'Hostilities Only' duties were not released until two years *after* the official end of hostilities. This eventually led to a sense of grievance among men anxious to return to their careers and on at least one ship, the *Leander*, a group of seamen took the highly illegal step of writing to a Member of Parliament protesting at the slow rate of demobilization. Whether their protest reached the Board of Admiralty will never be known. But it is a fact that, a few days later, the Board took the quite surprising decision to send out a signal to the Mediterranean Fleet to be posted on all ships' notice boards, pointing out the reasons why some men's release had to be delayed, and apologizing for the situation. The eventual speed-up came too late to save the men of the *Saumarez* and *Volage*; a tragically high proportion of the killed and wounded were youngsters just waiting for their demobilization numbers to come up.

There were swimming parties to the spacious beaches and the rocky coves around Corfu town; there was sun-bathing and water polo. But generally Jack amused himself as he has always done when in foreign parts, drinking in the local bars and eyeing the local girls. There were places in Corfu town, among those dim and dusty arcades in the old quarter, where girls waited for sailors far away from home and their own girl friends.

On 22 October the four ships were due to leave for what were described as 'exercises at sea'. Then the ships would rejoin the rest of the Mediterranean Fleet at the planned rendezvous—the bay of Argostoli on the Island of Cephalonia —for the annual Fleet Regatta, a kind of Oxford and Cambridge boat race multiplied a hundredfold. Every ship from the fleet would enter teams to row the ships' boats against each other. Seamen, telegraphists, stokers, signalmen, every section of the ships' companies would have their crews, even the cooks and officers' stewards whose duties were usually far removed from the art of seamanship.

The long-service sailors, who remembered the Fleet Regattas from before the war, regaled the just-out-of-school ordinary seamen with marvellous tales. Why, they would say, everyone gets the day off and each ship has its own Tote where you can place your bets (modest on a sailor's pay in 1946). And, the old shellbacks added, a kind of carnival air about the whole fleet seemed to relax discipline a little. Onerous things like 'rig of the day', the strict adherence to proper uniform at all times, were forgotten. Wear what you like! And some of the more adventurous ratings had been known to address officers by their Christian names (junior officers, mind you) and get away with it!

Yes, it would be great at Argostoli. And let's enjoy the last night in Corfu, because Malta with its boring routine of paint ship, clean ship, was not far away. It was understandable, perhaps, that the shore patrols from the ships, marching in threes through the town, had more than usual on which to cast a cold eye. As the boats drew into the jetty to take the shore-leave men back to their ships it was clear that many a youngster, unused to the fiery local *ouzo*, had overindulged, as indeed had many an old hand who should have known better.

One Petty Officer of many years service was seen making a determined yet not entirely controlled dash to catch the last liberty boat leaving the harbour for H.M.S. *Leander*. It was pulling away from the jetty just as he arrived, cap askew and panting heavily. He made a valiant leap for the stern, but his judgment of distance had obviously been impaired by the night's drinking and he fell with a shout and a splash between the jetty and the boat's stern. The howls of delight as the bedraggled Petty Officer was hauled aboard can easily be imagined.

As the fleet of liberty boats chugged across the harbour towards the four ships, there was one more indication that tomorrow they would all be leaving Corfu. H.M.S. *Mauritius*, now the flag ship of Rear-Admiral Kinahan, was a blaze of light. Drifting across the dark waters of the harbour came the sound of the Royal Marine band, relieved for once of the martial part of their repertoire, playing the light music popular at the time. Admiral Kinahan was giving a farewell party for the civic dignitaries of Corfu, one of those social occasions which are a traditional part of a peacetime Royal Navy Fleet. Beneath the canvas awning on the scrubbed quarter deck the ladies of Corfu and their gentlemen mixed with officers of the four ships. It was a colourful scene. Bunting used for signalling was wrapped round the stanchions supporting the awning. The sailmaker and his assistants had draped a red and white canopy beneath the awning. Some years later, one of the officers at that party, Lieut Keppel Edge-Partington of HMS *Saumarez*, was to recall: 'Had they [the officers] known what trials and tribulations lay in store for them during the next twenty-four hours they would have been more careful in their indulgences the night before.'*

* Now Capt Edge-Partington, retired; from an article in the *Gazette of the Joint Services Staff College*, 1956.

There had been another very good reason for the merry-making that night, for apart from saying farewell to the people of Corfu, it was 21 October—Trafalgar Day—the day the Royal Navy celebrates the famous victory in 1805 of its most famous sailor. No one aboard the four ships anchored in Corfu on Trafalgar Night could know that tomorrow they would witness one of the most ignominious defeats ever inflicted on the Navy. They were to lose eighty-four men killed or wounded and have two ships severely damaged. They would never see the enemy and not one of the four ships would fire a shot. And all this while facing a nation which did not even possess a Navy.

The morning of 22 October broke grey and dull. Low clouds covered the mountain peaks and swirled down the valleys of the Albanian coast. Throughout the forenoon the well-rehearsed routine for preparing ships for sea went ahead.

There was nothing to hint to the crews that they were preparing for anything other than a simple 150-mile passage to Argostoli to join the rest of the fleet for the regatta. Only Admiral Kinahan, the captains of the four ships and other key men knew the truth. The decision taken in London to test the strength of Albania's defiance had been translated into detailed and highly secret orders. The captains had opened their orders, marked XCU,* telling them that, instead of turning south on leaving Corfu, they were to steam through the North Corfu Channel, past the Albanian shore batteries. And if they were fired on they must fire back.

The capstans turned slowly as the cables were shortened, ready for the order to weigh anchor. The familiar throb pulsed gently through the ship as the stokers raised steam. On deck, the ships' cranes hoisted on board the last of the fresh food. The sea boats in which zealous crews had been practising for the regatta were run up into their davits. Finally the ships' motor boats, the last of their shore-bound errands completed, were hoisted. The ships were, in all respects, ready for sea. At

* Initials standing for Exercise Corfu, the code name given to the operation.

1.30 p.m. they steamed out of Corfu harbour. And aboard the flagship the duty signalman trained his lamp on the Corfu signal station to send farewell messages. Hundreds of islanders stood on the harbour walls to watch and wave as the ships, signal pennants stiff in the freshening wind, steamed out of harbour. It was an impressive sight. No one could know that, in a little over thirteen hours, two of those fine ships would be back in Corfu harbour; the *Saumarez* a smoking, wallowing, fire-blackened hulk with her dead and wounded lying on the twisted decks; the *Volage* forty feet shorter than when she left, and eight of her crew blown to pieces along with her bows.

Outside the harbour the ships took up their allotted stations for the passage through the North Channel. They were arranged in two groups. In the lead was the flagship *Mauritius*, followed by *Saumarez* 500 yards astern. Then, after an interval of two miles, came *Leander*, with *Volage* following in her wake at a distance of 500 yards. All the ships were steaming in line ahead. It was about this time that the ships' companies first learned that they were not to steam straight to Argostoli.

Aboard all four ships the captains went to the Tannoy broadcasting systems to speak to the ships' companies. The author remembers vividly the moment when the captain of H.M.S. *Leander*, Captain R. J. O. Otway-Ruthven, spoke, for it is not often in peacetime that one hears the words that so often presage trouble ahead: 'This is the captain speaking.' Captain Otway-Ruthven told the ship's company about the shelling of the *Orion* and *Superb* by the Albanians five months previously (for many of the crew it was the first they had heard about it) and went on: 'We are now about to pass through the same waters. If the shore batteries fire on us we will fire back, and we will not leave until every one is silenced.'

As he stepped away from the broadcasting microphone a Royal Marine bugler stepped forward to sound 'Action Stations'. Immediately each ship buzzed with two new sounds—the hum of startled, apprehensive conversation and the rattle of shoes on steel stairways and ladders as, throughout the ships, men went to action stations 'at the double'. The

25

youngsters who had never seen any action grabbed the nearest regular serving man and ĭsked, 'What do you reckon is going to happen?' And the regulars, pleased with the chance of showing off an air of blasé nonchalance, replied 'Not a bloody thing, sunshine. Who's going to mess about with us?' A good question. It is arguable that not one man of the 2,000 aboard the four ships, from the Admiral downwards, really believed that the Albanians would 'start anything'. The business with *Orion* and *Superb* was just an accident. Mistaken identity. The commander of the shore batteries must have been drunk.

By now the four ships were in the centre of the swept channel, one mile wide and ten miles long, which led through the narrows between Corfu and Albania and out, through the North Channel, to the open sea.

The navigating officers on each ship kept a careful watch on the bearings, and on the Mediterranean Routeing Instruction (known as Medri notices for short). These were issued by the Mediterranean Zone Mine Clearance Board (the Medzon Board) which had the task of finding and sweeping the thousands of mines laid by both sides during the war. Wherever possible, they cleared a corridor through a minefield, or confirmed that a previously swept corridor was still clear, and then returned later to sweep away all the mines. When a channel was known to be clear Medri notices, giving the routes to be followed through the mines, were issued to all nations.

As the four ships sailed carefully along the Medri route that afternoon all guns were trained fore and aft, the normal position for a passage at sea in peacetime, so as not to be overtly provocative.

But each gun turret had shells ready in the hoists. The sight of these shells, and the guns with their breeches open ready to receive them, must have convinced many a youngster in a gun's crew that he might see some real action at last.

That moment seemed very near when, soon after leaving Corfu, the *Volage* reported that a machine gun located on the Albanian shore appeared to have fired a burst at the destroyer. The Captain was ordered not to fire back unless he was absolutely certain that the action was deliberately offensive. The *Volage*'s guns remained silent.

Fifty miles to the north spotter planes took off from the aircraft carrier *Ocean* and headed for the Corfu Channel. Officially *Ocean* was cruising in the open sea ready to rendezvous with the four ships for 'Fleet exercises' on the way to Argostoli. In fact her real purpose in the vicinity was much more serious. The British Government, while it remained firm in its resolve to fire back if Admiral Kinahan's ships were fired on, was anxious to reduce to the minimum the danger of civilian casualties in that event. The spotter planes were ordered to patrol over the North Channel and, if the Albanians opened fire, report the position of the gun flashes to Admiral Kinahan. The Navy's answering shells could then be aimed directly at the gun emplacements.

On the bridges of the four ships dozens of pairs of binoculars scanned the Albanian shore, coming nearer every minute as the coast-line narrowed to the three-mile-wide bottleneck south of Saranda. As the *Mauritius*, still leading the line, moved through the narrows, the Medri Channel took her to within a mile of the Albanian coast, just as it had done for the *Superb* and the *Orion*, but from the opposite direction. It was known that the gun, or guns, which had fired on the Navy in May were sited on Limioni Hill, above Saranda. And, since that incident, Naval Intelligence had been endeavouring to discover the location of other coastal batteries.

To any commander in any service, an unprovoked act of war, as the shelling certainly was, evokes one simple reaction: discover and plot the source of the offence, in case of future retaliation. Naval Intelligence, without a doubt, followed this maxim. At the subsequent sessions of the International Court of Justice at The Hague great play was made by M Cot and his assistants of the fact that the Navy's *XCU* secret orders contained detailed positions of known gun batteries on the Albanian shore. Why should the knowledge of these positions be acquired by devious means unless it be with a view to offensive operations against them?

Events had persuaded the Admiralty that it was necessary deliberately to put four Royal Naval vessels in the sights of these guns to see if the Albanians would offend once again. The Admiralty would have been lacking in its duty if it had not taken steps to locate the batteries involved, and to inform the ships' captains. 'Forewarned is forearmed' is not, in situations such as these, a trite phrase.

In this respect the author has some interesting evidence of the lengths to which the Admiralty went to confirm its suspicions of Albania's total involvement in the firing on the *Orion* and the *Superb*. I have received evidence, clear and categoric, if unconfirmed, from a Royal Marine who was a member of Admiral Kinahan's staff aboard H.M.S. *Mauritius*. He was also—and this fact is of greater significance—a member of the Admiral's staff aboard the *Orion* when the *Orion* and the *Superb* made the North to South passage through the channel in May. His duties were to act as a messenger to the Admiral on the bridge, and when ashore, to be the Admiral's driver. He recalls quite clearly what happened when the *Orion* reached Corfu harbour after being shelled:

> We carried a jeep on board for the Admiral's use. On reaching harbour this was hoisted on to a barge and taken ashore. As soon as I had the jeep ready on the jetty, the Staff Officer Operations, a lieutenant-commander on the Admiral's staff, came ashore with a long object, well wrapped up, which he put into the back of the jeep. He got into the jeep with me, opened a map, told me to drive off and he would give me directions as we went along. After leaving Corfu town we kept to cart tracks all the time. The S.O.O. did everything possible to keep out of sight of people and places. We eventually stopped behind a long hedge and he then unwrapped his long parcel, which turned out to be the ship's main telescope.
>
> He stayed watching through the telescope for about ten minutes, then returned to the jeep and said 'Let's get out of here'. On returning to the jetty (at Corfu) he said to

28

me: 'I expect you can guess where we have been.' So I took it that we had been to that part of the island which is closest to Albania.

Thus it was that the gunnery officers and the captains of each of the four ships knew in which direction to train their guns if the telltale flashes were seen from the Albanian shore. It was now 2.25 p.m. almost an hour since the ships had left Corfu. The *Mauritius* and the *Saumarez* had passed through the narrowest part of the channel, still steaming line ahead at ten knots, down the centre of the mineswept corridor. In a few minutes Admiral Kinahan would give the order for a 'Turn' flag to be hoisted up the cruiser's mast, and the two leading warships would swing away from Saranda. On the bridge of the *Saumarez* Captain Selby kept his binoculars trained on the flag deck of the *Mauritius*, although casting an occasional checking glance on the gyro compass to make sure that the officer of the watch, Lieut Walter Godsal,* was keeping the destroyer accurately on course in the wake of the *Mauritius*. Lieut Godsal was to recall later: 'There was no danger of my slipping up. As we left harbour Captain Selby threatened me with fates worse than death if I let the ship veer from the proper course.'

At this stage it is worth while to analyse briefly the background and characters of the destroyers' captains, Selby of the *Saumarez*, and Paul of the *Volage*. For, as the ships ploughed steadily on, the two men were only minutes from the moment when each would face the most agonizing hours of their careers. Their characters, skill and experience would be tested and probed with a severity which would reveal the slightest weakness; they were to emerge with all those qualities intact and enhanced to a high degree.

The two men were dissimilar in every way except for their skill as seamen. Captain W. H. Selby was a stocky man of average height and a strict disciplinarian (as befits a flotilla commander), a man who was not averse to calling a spade a

* Now Captain Godsal, serving at the Admiralty Under-Water Establishment, Portland.

bloody shovel if it would make his comments the more effective. He was a professional destroyer man and the *Saumarez* was his seventh destroyer command. Like all destroyer men, from ordinary seaman to captain, he looked upon 'big ship sailors', the officers and men of the cruisers, battleships and aircraft carriers, with a benign tolerance.

This attitude, and his down-to-earth approach which endeared him to his crew, is best illustrated by an incident recalled by one of his senior ratings. On one occasion *Saumarez* had the unusual distinction of having to secure alongside the flagship of the Commander-in-Chief in Grand Harbour, Malta. Captain Selby, concerned about his 'small ship' sailors and the 'big ship' men coming into such close proximity, gave the whole ship's company a lecture on how to behave while under the eye of the C-in-C.

'The Admiral isn't a destroyer man like me,' said Captain Selby. 'So, as you move around the upper deck, I want none of your effing this and effing that and effing the other.' It is certain that, after a life-time at sea, Admiral Willis needed no shielding from forthright sailor language, but Captain Selby was leaving nothing to chance where the reputation of his ship was concerned.

Commander Reginald Paul of the *Volage* was a tall, thick-set man. His background was certainly an unusual one for a Commander in the Royal Navy. He was a first class musician, playing both the piano and the organ, and a linguist of note, speaking French, Italian and German fluently. The *Volage* was his first command and his progress towards that proud moment was through the technical branches of radio communications and electronics, rather than the upper deck world of seamanship, which is the usual route by which officers progress towards command. Few officers have had their arts of seamanship tested as severely as did Commander Paul that day.

At 2.47 p.m. *Mauritius* signalled a turn to port and swung left on to the new course—310 degrees, roughly north-west—carefully following the Medri Channel as it stretched towards the open sea. Aboard *Saumarez* Captain Selby gave the orders

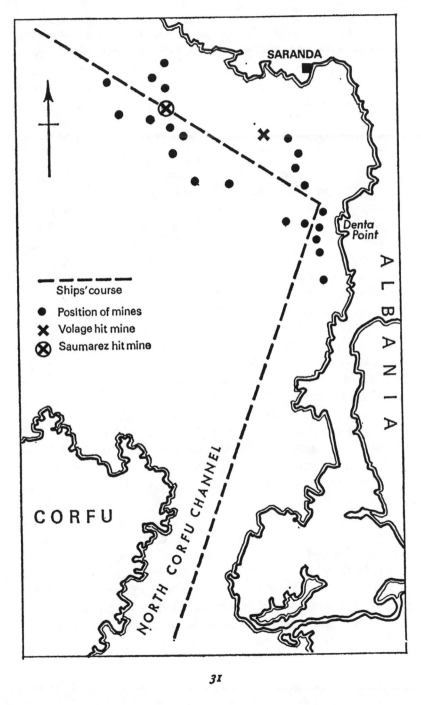

SARANDA

Denta
Point

A L B A N I A

Ships' course
● Position of mines
✕ Volage hit mine
⊗ Saumarez hit mine

CORFU

NORTH CORFU CHANNEL

that kept the ship dead astern of the *Mauritius*. Two miles back the *Leander* and the *Volage* prepared to make the same manoeuvre on reaching the same position. Aboard the ships a feeling of anti-climax was affecting everyone as they swung away from the known positions of the Albanian shore batteries. The youngsters aboard were becoming resigned to the fact that they would not get their first taste of hostile action after all; the regular sailors were saying: 'Told you so; this Action Stations business is just a sky-lark.'

It happened six minutes after *Saumarez* had begun steering her new course, at 2.53 p.m. precisely. A colossal explosion erupted beneath the ship a few feet forward of the bridge, sending the bows rearing into the air. A brilliant yellow flash shot up vertically from the port side, followed almost simultaneously by another yellow flash leaping out horizontally on the starboard side as the explosion ripped through compartment after compartment across the whole of the ship. In a split second a thirty-foot section of the destroyer from the keel to just below the bridge was reduced to a mass of tangled, twisted metal. The explosion tore down compartment walls made of quarter-inch steel; it flung massive, water-tight doors against bulkheads as though they were plywood. And then a tongue of yellow flame flashed through this shambles, searing everything, human or man-made, which stood in its path.

The explosion had ripped out the starboard side of the ship below the bridge and the water rushed in. Huge areas of the fore-part of the ship which, a second ago, had been entirely secure, sealed off in their separate compartments, were now open to the in-rushing seas. Water-tight doors, apparently intact but in fact weakened by the explosion, groaned and finally gave way before the mounting pressure of the water. The blast ripped open the main fuel tanks and the thick, black oil spurted out and was carried by the tidal wave of water through the wrecked compartments, adding the menace of fire to a ship which already seemed mortally stricken as she began to settle ominously by the bows. Everywhere, from the forward boiler room to the radio room, the transmitting station, from the magazine where ammunition for the Bofors guns was stored to the bridge itself, from the keel to the flag deck, was a shambles.

On the bridge the force of the explosion blew the officers, the look-outs and the signalmen into a tangle of bodies on the deck. A huge water spout thrown up by the explosion picked up great gulps of fuel oil and twisted wreckage on the way and then dropped on to the open bridge, drenching everyone.

As the roar of the explosion was rumbling around the Albanian hills, as the ship reared and lurched against the force of the blast, a new sound took over and filled the air with its banshee wailings—the ship's siren. It drowned the cries of the wounded, many of them so badly hurt they would be dead before it stopped. It drowned the welter of noise which, after the initial split-second of shocked silence, broke out, a noise made up of cries of alarm, questioning profanities, firm voices of command.

On the bridge of the flagship, as all heads swung to look astern as the explosion was heard, it seemed this new noise was an intentional distress signal. But there was no need for that; distress was to be seen in the huge plume of black smoke belching from the *Saumarez* and her rapidly worsening list.

As the *Saumarez* officers on the bridge picked themselves up, the siren wailed on and on. They looked in the direction of the siren, which was fixed behind the funnel, but could not see it because the mast and the funnel itself blocked their line of vision. Someone went to investigate, and reported back. A piece of metal, sucked up in the water spout caused by the explosion, had fallen on the siren and wrapped itself around the lanyard, triggering off the blast of steam by which it was activated.

It was too high up for anyone to reach· but gradually the noise grew quieter and quieter. The engines were beginning to fail as the steam which drove them, and the siren, faltered and finally gave out in the shattered Number One boiler room. The ship lost way and lay wallowing, her nose nestling in the troughs of the waves, shattered and helpless. And now, where there had been noise and commotion, there was silence. No throb of engines, no wind sighing through rigging and halyards, just the lop, lop, of a lazy sea against her shattered sides—and the cries of the wounded.

Up on the bridge Captain Selby staggered to his feet, and shouted into the voice pipe which connected the bridge with the wheelhouse below: 'Stop main engines. Report damage.' One man with a vivid recollection of what it was like on the bridge of the *Saumarez* at that moment is Mr E. G. Tunnicliffe, now a coastguard in Devon. At the time he was a very 'green' ordinary signalman, aged nineteen, only recently having completed his training. He was on duty on the starboard side of the flag deck when the *Saumarez* hit the mine. He recalls:

> I was looking through binoculars to the high land behind the town of Saranda, where someone had said they had seen men transporting shells to nearby guns. Then there was a sudden roar of noise and for a moment I thought I was under the water and coming up through it (I hoped) to the surface. Then I saw the Morse key which operated the signal lamp on the mast head and I realized that I was still on the flag deck and it was water and oil etc. *coming down* around me and not myself who was going up! I realized I was unhurt, but the person who was standing next to me (I cannot now remember who it was) had disappeared and I never saw him again.

Lieut Hugh Knollys, the navigator, also has a vivid memory of those horrifying seconds immediately after the explosion, which blew him fifteen feet from the compass platform and left him draped, badly hurt and unconscious, over a signal projector on the starboard wing of the bridge. And one of his recollections underlines the quality which never deserts the British serviceman, even in a moment of great trial and mortal danger, his sense of humour.

> I remember 'coming to' almost immediately after the explosion and, under the impression that we had been

fired on by the shore batteries, I crawled back on to the compass platform and rammed a tin hat on to my head. I looked up and saw the Chief Yeoman of Signals standing over me. 'I should sit on that if I were you, sir,' he said. 'It wasn't a shell. It was a mine.'

Up in the director control tower, above and immediately abaft the bridge, the gunnery officer, Lieut Peter Wells-Cole, suffered particularly from being in a confined space. His head was only inches from the deckhead of the director and the force of the explosion lifted him vertically upwards. He was knocked unconscious, but eventually made his way to the bridge and, although in a dazed condition, appeared to be unhurt. It was to take two days for the truth to come out.

Lieut the Hon Terence Stopford, the torpedo officer, emerged unscathed from the tangle of bodies on the bridge. He dashed down the bridge ladder and saw two men coming from the main damage area, supporting a third man between them. He was obviously badly wounded. As they staggered with the wounded man towards the sick bay one of the men said, 'There's another one trapped in one of the forward mess decks, sir. We could hear him shouting.'

Stopford raced forward and went down the hatchway ladder to the forward messdeck. He could see no sign of anyone trapped. Then he heard a thin cry. It appeared to be coming from below his feet. There was another messdeck immediately below and Stopford, bumping and jarring himself against furniture and equipment in the darkness, eventually found the hatchway which led down the lower messdeck. What he saw made him doubt his own eyes. The messdeck was obviously flooded. Black, oily water lapped against the coaming around the hatchway. That meant the messdeck must be flooded to within an inch or two of the deckhead. How could anyone be alive and calling for help from in there? He was about to turn away and search elsewhere when he heard the cry again. Again it appeared to be coming from beneath his feet, but much closer this time. He knelt down by the hatchway, his face just above the oily water, and listened. A few seconds later he heard the cry once again. There *was* someone down there, and not very far from the hatch.

Lying on his stomach Stopford thrust his arm as far as he could inside the messdeck and eventually touched a body. The man, trapped by the water which had filled the messdeck, was now jammed against the deckhead. By pushing his face against the deckhead, he was able to get a few gulps of air. Blinded by the darkness, and by his fear and panic, he did not realize he was only a few feet from safety.

Stopford tried to pull him towards the hatchway, but the man seemed unwilling, or unable, to help himself. Stopford then urged him to duck down under the surface of the water and he would try to pull him up again through the hatch. But the man could not bring himself to abandon the pocket of air which was keeping him alive, but which could not be expected to do so for much longer. His life now depended on whether Stopford could pull him through the water to the hatchway. He shouted to the man to take a deep breath and then, taking as firm a grip as he could, Stopford pulled with all his strength.

The task seemed hopeless. The man was either jammed tight against the deckhead or, in his panic-stricken state, he was holding on to something. The seconds ticked away as Stopford heaved once again. This time he felt a movement and, with a final pull, the man's head broke the surface of the water. He was alive, but utterly unable to help himself. After a few seconds rest to get his own breath back, Stopford put his arms under the man's arm-pits and, bracing his legs, hauled him out of the water. They both collapsed on the deck by the side of the hatchway.

He still had to get the man through the messdeck and up a gangway ladder to the upper deck. He explained that he was going to fetch help but the man, a stoker petty officer, clung to him and cried: 'Don't leave me, sir! Please don't leave me!' Stopford tried to reassure the poor chap that he would come back with help, dragged himself free of the man's grip and climbed the ladder to the upper deck.

There, standing on the wing of the bridge above him and only a few yards away, was Peter Wells-Cole, looking directly at him. Stopford shouted, 'Come and give me a hand.' But Wells-Cole continued to stare straight at him and took no notice. Stopford shouted again, but again there was no reaction. He looked around for someone else to help him, but there was no one near at hand.

He returned to the messdeck alone and somehow managed to haul the man up the ladder to the upper deck. He had severe internal injuries, but he survived. He was eventually moved to Bighi Hospital in Malta and Stopford visited him there. Stopford recalls: 'His gratitude was quite embarrassing.'

The First Lieutenant of *Saumarez*, Lieut E. F. Gueritz,* had just completed his rounds of the ship to make sure that everything and everyone was in a full state of preparedness when the explosion came. He was no stranger to violent action, as the ribbon of the Distinguished Service Cross on his jacket and the rosette which denotes a Bar to the award, testified.

Gueritz had just climbed the ladder to the bridge when the ship heaved under the explosion. His first recollection was of seeing Lieut Edge-Partington blown into the air and thinking, 'I hope he doesn't come down on top of me; he's quite a heavy chap.' Edge-Partington fell on to something much harder, the metal deck, and was virtually *hors de combat* for the rest of the day.

Another officer on the bridge, Lieut the Hon John Edmondson,† was blown against the torpedo deflection sight and knocked unconscious. He, too, was unable to play much part in the subsequent happenings.

But was it a mine which had caused the disaster? In those first chaotic minutes after the explosion, no one could be entirely sure. Certainly danger from mines had never been

* He retired in 1972 with the rank of Rear-Admiral. His last appointment was Commandment of the Joint Warfare Establishment, Old Sarum, Wiltshire.

† Now Baron Sandford of Banbury, a Minister in the Department of the Environment. He served through the war and was wounded during the Normandy landings. He retired from the Royal Navy in 1956, when he was Commander of the Home Fleet flagship, H.M.S. *Tyne*.

contemplated, and neither of the cruisers had its minesweeping gear out. Everyone had thought that the danger, if it came, would be from the shore batteries.

Then other thoughts began to creep in. No great activity had been seen around the shore batteries. No one on the upper deck of any of the four ships had seen the flash of gunfire or heard the scream of shells. Could it have been a torpedo fired from a fixed tube on the Albanian shore? This theory was discounted by the fact that no one had seen the track of a torpedo heading for the destroyer.

It did not take Captain Selby long to realize the truth. The vast power of the explosion, the fact that even by a quick inspection of the damage he could see that the blast had been well below the water line, the tell-tale waterspout shooting vertically into the air—all these things told the man who had been bombed and shelled on destroyers throughout the war that his ship had struck a mine of considerable power almost underneath her keel, and therefore at a depth of eleven feet. There was little doubt in his mind as he reported to the flag-ship: 'I have been mined forward.'

Most of the bridge party were in a dazed and shocked condition. But years of experience and training led everyone to do what he should do in an emergency, which of course is the ultimate object of all training. Captain Selby's order to 'Stop the main engines. Report damage,' when he staggered from the floor of the bridge was an automatic reaction; he could see the crippled *Saumarez*, her engines dying, was heaving to of her own accord. The reply from the wheelhouse could hardly have been more serious. The coxswain reported that the steering and the engine room telegraphs were out of action. Captain Selby ordered the wheelhouse crew to abandon their position and man the emergency conning position, and report back to him when communications had been established.

Similarly, Lieut Knollys reacted automatically. As navigating officer, it was his immediate duty to fix the position where the ship had met with disaster. As he dragged himself back on to the compass platform he found that the compass had been blown out of its gimbals—the mountings which allow it to swing so that bearings can be taken. But the position where the *Saumarez* hit the mine was accurately recorded by another officer who also acted automatically—Lieut-Commander Lankester, the squadron navigating officer responsible for the navigation planning of the four ships.

On hearing the explosion astern of the *Mauritius* he swung round and picked up the *Saumarez* in his binoculars. He quickly took a fix on her position and then, to make sure there was no room for doubt, he checked his findings by a second navigational method. The result was to be vital, damning evidence against Albania. Lieut-Commander Lankester's careful reckoning placed the *Saumarez* almost due north of the Barchetta Rock, a well known navigational mark off the north-east corner of Corfu Island, and three and nine-tenths miles from the Rock. This position was almost in the centre of the supposedly mine-free channel.

As Admiral Kinahan considered this chilling information, the extent of the damage to the *Saumarez* was being revealed as officers and men from the shattered area of the vessel made their reports to the bridge. The point of impact seemed to be the bulkhead dividing Number Five fuel tank on the starboard side from Number One boiler room immediately astern of it.

The force of the explosion coming from a distance of mere feet ripped open the five other fuel tanks which stretched across the complete width of the ship from port to starboard. The tank covers were blown out of their mountings and oil burst up through the shattered decks above the tanks, carrying the oil to the compartments and passageways above the explosion area in the wake of the blast.

Number One boiler room, immediately behind the fuel tanks, also took the main force of the explosion. This compartment, which also stretched the width of the ship, became a sudden and terrifying holocaust as the mine blew in the starboard side of the compartment and then blew out the opposite side.

There are no eye-witness accounts of what must have been a terrifying scene in the boiler room below the ship's waterline.

The reason is tragic in its simplicity—all the five men on duty in the boiler room perished and their bodies were never recovered. The only comfort which remains is in the fact that death came quickly. The Number Two boiler room and the engine room, astern of the main area of the explosion, remained intact, but the crews in these two compartments had reason to wonder how they had escaped death or serious injury. We have seen how the force of the explosion, coming from underneath the ship, lifted officers and men on the bridge off their feet and flung them into the air. The bridge was the highest manned area of the ship, as far above the explosion as it was possible to be. It can, therefore, be easily imagined how much more violent was the force of the explosion in the engine room and Number Two boiler room, which were so much nearer the explosion, and were also confined compartments which did not allow the force of the blast to escape into the open air.

Engine Room Artificer F. W. H. Spiller was one of the engineering staff on duty in Number Two boiler room that afternoon. He vividly remembers what happened, although we will see that only chance decreed that he was to live to be able to recount the story, and another man was to die in his place.

> We were steaming along quite happily when I suddenly found myself falling from about eight feet in the air with the boiler room plates also falling just below me. I remember thinking to myself: 'I hope those plates fall flat.' They did, and I got away with minor rib injuries.

The plates to which Spiller refers are the gratings which surround all the machinery in the two boiler rooms and the engine room. They are of heavy metal, slotted into steel frameworks, and crews move around the machinery on them, checking the gauges and throttles. They are made in sections so that they can be removed to get at the bilges beneath them for cleaning out the oil and water which accumulates. If anyone in the boiler room or engine room had been hit by the edge of those flying plates he would certainly have been killed or seriously wounded.

But Spiller had a second reason to be thankful for his life, the fact that he should not have been in Number Two boiler room at all. His regular action station was in Number One boiler room and, as he picked himself up from the deck, one name flashed through his mind—Willie Ford. A glance at the steam pressure gauges monitored from Number One boiler room showed that pressure there was falling ominously. That meant the main damage was in Number One boiler room and Willie Ford, just twenty-one years of age, had only two hours earlier swopped action stations with Spiller. Twenty-five years after the incident Spiller still feels emotional as he remembers how it happened.

> Willie Ford joined the ship as a young engine room artificer, fifth class, for experience, and to get his boiler room and engine room watchkeeping certificates, and he spent quite a lot of time with me watchkeeping in the engine room. He was very keen and interested in all aspects of engine room duties, but his real love was diesel engines. In *Saumarez* we had a diesel engine as an emergency generator in Number One boiler room. At 'Action Stations' it was the practice to start up this engine in case it was needed. On this fateful day young Willie decided he would like to take over my 'Action Station' in the Number One boiler room, so that he could 'run up' the diesel engine all on his own. He asked the permission of his Chief Engine Room Artificer to change positions with me.

With a matter-of-fact finality which fails to hide the emotion he still feels, Spiller concludes: 'This request was granted—and we never saw Willie again. So *I* am writing this letter to you.'* Young Willie Ford, from Devon, died with the rest of the crew in Number One boiler room, tending his beloved diesel engine.

* In a letter to the author.

41

In the engine room immediately behind Number Two boiler room, Engineer Lieut Jack Shackleton was on the control platform with Engine Room Artificer Griffiths immediately before the explosion. When the blast hit them they were thrown four feet into the air and fell back on to the engine room plates in a heap of twisted, tangled bodies. As they picked themselves up, badly bruised and shaken, there were cries of, 'Anyone hurt? Everyone all right?'

Lieut Shackleton could see nothing but a dense, swirling, choking fog that gripped his throat and stung his eyes. The engine room was filled with black, oily dust which the explosion had blown from those inaccessible places in the engine room where it had settled, well beyond the reach of a stoker's cleaning rag. Gradually the fog settled and the engine room crew could see the dim glimmer of the lights.

They staggered on to the control platform and saw that the steam gauge for Number One boiler which, until seconds ago had been registering the required 300 pounds of pressure, was 'walking back'. Slowly, as the pressure failed, the needle slipped farther and farther back until it registered zero. Lieut Shackleton grabbed the power-pack telephone and wound the handle to contact Number One boiler room. Again and again the handle whirred, but there was no answer. The sea was already rushing into the boiler room from both sides of the ship. Oil from the fractured fuel tanks spurted everywhere. And the water with its slimy coating of oil rose inexorably until the boiler room was flooded to the level of the sea outside.

The engine room crew shut down on the throttles and isolated the useless Number One boiler room. Number Two boiler room reported that they had full working steam pressure of 300 pounds. They tried to get the ship moving ahead again but the state of the ship with its severe list and hundreds of tons of water rushing inboard, was more than the power from one boiler could deal with, and the pressure began to fall away. Then sea water contamination from Number One boiler room got into the water supplying Number Two boiler, the pressure failed once again and finally the pressure gauge on Number Two boiler 'walked back' to zero.

Both engines were now stationary and this brought an eerie new situation which, following on the cataclysmic events of the first few minutes, might well have carried the threat of panic to a crew containing a high proportion of youngsters who had never known any kind of offensive action. As the second engine failed, so the turbo-generator which supplied all the electric power for the destroyer, began to die.

Under normal conditions it operated with a constant, comforting high-pitched whine. But the power for the generator was supplied by the main engines, and the generator's whine became lower and lower as the turbines slowed. As one man in the engine room at the time said: 'It was like an old-fashioned gramophone running down because the spring had not been wound up.'

As the generator ran down, so the lights throughout the ship began to get dimmer and failed completely when the generator finally stuttered to a halt. Now the only lights in the ship were the dim emergency lamps. In the parts of the ship shattered, or badly damaged, by the explosion, there was no light at all. It was also strangely silent, for the generator supplied the fans which pumped air to every part of the ship. Now the fans had stopped. The ever-present sounds of the gentle rumble of air in the ventilation trunking, and the quiet hiss of air escaping from a vent or two, died away.

Then, borne on this unaccustomed silence, came sounds which were to bring the *Saumarez* to her greatest peril, and some members of her crew to deaths fearful to contemplate. With a sudden flash and roar, the oil from the fractured fuel tanks caught fire. A huge, black belch of smoke burst from the destroyer's shattered sides and spiralled skywards.

It is not certain, even now, what caused the ignition. It could have been the flash of the original explosion, although many of the survivors recall a short lapse of time between the explosion and the outbreak of the fire. It could have been caused by oil fuel from the tanks being flung against the

Number One boiler, and eventually ignited by the boiler's heat. But one thing is certain; when the fire did burst out it spread with terrifying speed. It raced through compartments opened up by the explosion, from the Number One boiler room and the fuel tanks to the compartments immediately beneath the bridge structure. It burst forward through compartment after compartment, along passageway after passageway, fed by the oil fuel which the explosion had flung over the twisted metal and buckled bulkheads.

At the moment of the explosion there were many men between decks in this forward section of the ship. They were damage control parties, groups of two or three men, stationed at intervals throughout the ship to be ready to give effective and immediate action if the ship were damaged in any way. This is normal routine in the Royal Navy when a ship goes to Action Stations and also, which automatically follows, to its highest degree of damage control preparedness.

We have seen how the blast blew men up to eight feet in the air on the bridge and in the engine and boiler compartments. The men in these positions were lucky. Those on the bridge were lifted into the air; their injuries were relatively minor and were caused not by being blown up but by hitting the deck or pieces of equipment as they came down. It was a similar situation in the engine room and Number Two boiler room. These compartments were among the biggest in the ship; they had to be to contain the massive boilers, the engines and all the ancillary equipment. Compared with other compartments they were like caverns, stretching in height from the bilges to the upper deck. When the mine exploded the crews were flung into the air, but again there was nothing above them which their bodies could hit and cause serious injury.

It was, alas, a tragically different story in the compartments and passageways above and forward of the immediate area of the explosion. Naval architects, when they are designing a ship, conserve space like a miser, whether the ship be a 30,000-ton battleship or a tiny frigate. Outside the main machinery section of any ship, the space between the floor and ceiling in any compartment or passageway rarely exceeds seven feet. When the explosion hit the *Saumarez* the members of the damage control parties in the immediate area of the explosion stood little chance of escaping death, or, at least, serious injury. The upward heave of the explosion, bursting through the decks beneath their feet, hurled them upwards. Men immediately about the point of impact were flung against a deckhead only inches away; many died from fractured skulls.

Others, in compartments farther away, were flung against bulkheads or pieces of machinery. Those too badly injured to crawl to safety and who were not rescued by parties even then being hurriedly formed, soon became victims of the fire or were trapped in compartments where the force of the explosion had buckled decks and bulkheads and jammed the heavy watertight doors.

Even now, when time has had the chance to dim and blur the memory, survivors who saw the terrible fate of many of their shipmates—and had to stand back helpless—cannot recall these incidents without emotion overcoming them.

One man, a petty officer torpedo-instructor aboard *Saumarez*, recalls how he found two electricians missing from their Action Stations and quickly ordered them to get 'closed up like everyone else'. He never saw them again—their Action Station was in the forward electrical switchboard, which was situated directly above the ruptured fuel oil tanks. He has no reason to feel responsibility for their deaths; he was doing his clear duty in ordering them to their Action Stations. But his account of the incident makes it quite clear that this is something he can never forget.

The senior ratings aboard *Saumarez* had been briefed the night before we sailed (21 October) that all hands would be at Action Stations. We were to be ready for anything. There was a lot of preparation that night in all departments of the ship making sure everything was on 'top line'. In the electrical department all the gun firing circuits had to be checked. We checked the emergency lighting circuits and all the communications. It was well after midnight before everything was satisfactory to me and my senior officer.

When we sailed for the Channel on the following morning I checked up by telephone to make sure that men in my department were at their Action Stations on the bridge, the after switchboard and the forward switchboard. I called each one in turn and all was well apart from the forward switchboard, where I got no reply. I went along to check, but the two ratings who should have been on duty there were missing. They had gone to the forward mess deck with the forward damage control party and someone had brewed up some tea. There was a lot of leg-pulling when I told these two ratings to get to their Action Stations position. They had served during the war and had seen action of one sort or another. This was peacetime. 'What the hell was there to worry about?' was the attitude they were adopting. However, I soon got these two ratings back down to the forward switchboard. I also checked there was someone in the gyro compass room.

I then proceeded up and out on to the upper deck by the starboard waist. There I met an engine room artificer who had been on the ship only a few days. He said the engine room fan was giving trouble and asked if I would get someone to work on it. I turned around to return forward when it all happened. It seemed as if I was enveloped in a ball of fire. When I 'came to' I was lying on the deck right back by the aft superstructure supporting 'X' gun. Beside me was the E.R.A., with a gash on his head and most of his clothing burned. I thought he was dead. He must have been tough. I gave him a good shake and he opened his eyes and said: 'What the hell hit us?'

We were both wet through; we had been drenched by the water spout from the explosion falling all over us. All my outer clothes were burned, even my socks. The skin on my face was burned and my hands were like scorched red meat. I had a tidy-sized lump on my head, caused when I was blown against the superstructure. I couldn't see very well because my eye-balls were scorched. All my body seemed to be on fire. But I was one of the lucky ones. What must the poor chaps who were really badly burned be feeling? What hell they must have gone through. Even now, after twenty-five years, I can still hear some of them screaming, and I remember later, aboard the hospital ship, how some of them fought for their lives.*

The letter then breaks off with a most poignant sentence: 'Excuse me, Sir, if I pack this in for this evening; it is not always good to recall some of these things.'

The following morning he resumed his account of the disaster just where it had been so abruptly suspended the evening before. He recalls that, as soon as he and the E.R.A. had recovered sufficiently they decided to go to their mess deck, which was away from the damage area, to get some clean clothing to put over their burns to keep out any infection. There was no suggestion in his account of the incident—and one is therefore certain that there was no thought in their minds—about going immediately to have their very serious burns treated. Each one had a job to do to try to save the crippled ship, and to help the trapped and the more seriously wounded.

Up on the deck again there was naturally some confusion, but things gradually began to get into some order. All electrical power had failed. An attempt to get an auxiliary dynamo started was unsuccessful. The forward damage control party were isolated for a time in the forward mess deck, but most of them managed to get up and out on to the upper deck, through the petty officers' mess, and started fighting the fires. One of my staff, a Leading Seaman Murphy, from the forward repair party,

* In a letter to the author.

told me all his lads were safe, but he was worried about the ratings in the forward switchboard and one in the gyro-room. By this time most of us realized we had hit a mine. Some of the lads of X-gun were really mad and wanted to open fire on the Albanian shore. But an officer came along and told them in no uncertain words not to be so stupid and to get on with fighting the fires and trying to get out some of the lads who were trapped. My lads had got one of the ratings out of the forward switchboard. He was in a terrible state and died late that evening. We could not find the rating in the gyro-room and he must have been killed. The second rating in the forward switchboard was safe because, luckily for him, he had gone to the lavatory just before the mine hit us.

I worried about the deaths of those two young ratings. Remember, I had ordered them to stay at their 'Action Stations'. One of them had been married before we left England and his wife was expecting a baby. These things flash through your mind. Some of the bodies and the injured were now being brought up from the compartments and passageways in the forward part of the ship, and laid down on the deck in the starboard waist near the torpedo tubes. It was an awful sight; burned flesh is not pretty.

Petty Officer Hodges, the submarine detection instructor, had been on the upper deck and close to the explosion area. He was flung against a bulkhead, but escaped injury. As he picked himself up' he saw one of the ship's cooks, who had been a member of a forward damage control party, emerging from between decks and staggering towards him. It was an experience which Hodges, and other crew members who witnessed the scene, can never forget. He was fearfully burned. All the clothing on the front of his body was burned away. His flesh was charred. And, as he staggered towards Hodges, he was crying plaintively, 'Help me, help me.' Mercifully, death soon released him from his agony.

Another man, driven to hysteria by his burns, was lying on the upper deck, hands outstretched, screaming 'Shoot me, somebody, shoot me.' Again, the release for which he pleaded was merciful in its speed.

Hodges went on a tour of the upper deck to see what help he could give to the wounded. On 'X' gun deck he found two men lying on the deck. They had been blown there by the explosion. One of them, a young seaman, was badly burned about the face. All his hair had gone and he had a broken jaw. He died the following day. The other man was a leading seaman, one of the coxswains of the destroyer's motor boat. He had severe internal injuries from which he died two days later. But at that moment, as Hodges knelt down beside him, he mustered the strength to smile wanly and say, 'I could do with my tot.'

By now the destroyer's tiny sick bay was filled and more and more wounded were laid down in the starboard waist, wrapped in blankets. For some little could be done; the blankets were pulled over their faces. The medical staff aboard the destroyer comprised a young doctor and an even younger sick berth attendant. Until help came from the *Volage* they struggled along with an overwhelming task. The doctor was Surgeon-Lieutenant O'Riordan, an Irishman serving in the Royal Naval Volunteer Reserve, and waiting for his release to take up a family practice.

His assistant, Sick Berth Attendant S. A. Mitchell was only eighteen years of age. He came from Scotland, had a mop of red hair and was known to the crew as 'Tiny', being little more than five feet tall. Throughout the day and the long night to come their unceasing care and concern for the wounded earned them the highest praise. For the men with severe burns there was little more they could do than give morphine injections to ease the pain, and to cover up the blistered areas of their bodies. The men with injuries caused by being flung against deckheads and bulkheads were given emergency treatment and made as comfortable as possible, but many of them urgently needed the resources which only a full-scale hospital could provide.

Now a new danger was added to the perils which menaced the destroyer—the oil escaping from her ruptured tanks and spreading across the sea around her caught fire. Within seconds most of the bow section of the destroyer, by now so low in the water that the seas almost splashed over it, was ringed with flames. More and more oil bubbled up from the tanks below the water line to feed the flames. It flashed through the mind of one officer aboard the *Saumarez* that oil which, poured on stormy water to calm down the waves had saved hundreds of lives at sea down the years might, cruelly and paradoxically, spell the final and terrible end for the destroyer and her crew.

Down below, stokers and engineering officers fought desperately to coax a little life from the engine—just enough power to allow her to steam away from the blazing oil would give her a reasonable chance of survival. But it was impossible. Sea water or air locks in the feed pipes to the boiler made the engines useless.

The flames had already blackened the sides of the bridge superstructure and the fierce fires in the compartments below the bridge now imperilled the nerve centre of the ship. Captain Selby decided that he had no option but to evacuate the bridge and transfer his command to the emergency conning position abaft the funnel. At this position, built for such an emegency, all the controls of the ship are duplicated, and here, or on the quarter deck, Captain Selby remained throughout the long night to come as the battle to save his ship went on.

But, in one respect, the drill of evacuating the bridge and taking up the new position was not carried out swiftly enough for him. When he arrived there he contacted the emergency conning position by voice pipe to make sure the coxswain was closed-up at the emergency wheel. When he was told the coxswain had not yet arrived he exclaimed angrily, 'Where the hell is he then?' He arrived a few seconds later, and Captain Selby learned why he had been rather slow. Both his ankles had been broken in the explosion. The chief quartermaster had, in the meantime, taken over his duties.

Aboard the *Mauritius*, which had stopped in the centre of the swept channel when *Saumarez* blew up, Rear-Admiral Kinahan peered at his shattered flotilla leader and tried to sum up the situation. For the *Saumarez* it appeared to be a desperate one. Her bows, sagging beneath the weight of the tons of water which now filled much of her forward section, were ringed with flame from the oil on the water. Occasionally bigger gusts of flame shot from the blazing fuel tanks. The huge column of black smoke rising above the destroyer drifted ominously towards the Albanian shore. The wind, freshening now, was blowing the helpless destroyer out of the swept channel towards the Albanian coast-line beneath the guns which still remained silent.

There was no doubt in anyone's mind now, certainly not in the mind of the Admiral, that it was indeed a hostile shore. Within five months two British cruisers had been fired on and the *Saumarez* had hit a mine in a channel marked 'safe' on the charts of ships of every maritime nation in the world. The coincidence was too great to be ignored. And one mine meant others; for no one ever laid a single mine. The fleeting thought that the damage might have been caused by a floating mine which had broken free from one of the war-time fields was at once dismissed by the fact that the centre of the damage was well below the water line.

The gun-crews of *Mauritius*, *Leander* and *Volage* waited eagerly for the order, which they were sure must come, to open fire. The order never came. The six-inch guns of the cruisers and the 4.7-inch guns of the *Volage* remained trained fore and aft, in accordance with Admiralty instructions that there should be no hint of provocation by the British ships. They were to fire back only if fired on from the shore. Admiral Kinahan obeyed his orders to the letter, as any other commander would have done in the same circumstances. The ships had not been *fired* on. There was, as yet, no *proof* that Albania was to blame for the laying of the mines.

But, as Admiral Kinahan looked at the drifting *Saumarez* through his binoculars and his officers on the bridge scanned the Albanian shore, one further factor added to the near-certainty of Albania's culpability—the complete and utter silence from the Albanian shore. No morse light flashed from the signal station high on Limioni Hill. No radio message was received offering assistance for the *Saumarez*, clearly visible to the watchers on the shore as she blazed and belched her plume of black smoke. No message had been received warning the ships that they were steaming into a minefield. By any civilized standards it was a display of callous disregard for human life at sea unequalled since the infamous wreckers put lights on rocky shores to lure ships to their doom and plunder their cargoes.

Admiral Kinahan put down his binoculars and began to issue his orders. He spoke firmly, but calmly, and to the young ratings on the bridge the very calmness of their senior officer seemed to add to the sense of unreality. It all sounded like an ordinary peacetime exercise at sea. To one man on the bridge 'it was difficult to believe that someone had blown up one of our ships, until you turned and looked astern and saw the flames and the smoke'.

Admiral Kinahan's first order was for the *Volage*, the last ship in the line and still some distance astern, to try to take the *Saumarez* in tow. The Admiral reasoned that the first and most pressing priority was to save the destroyer from drifting on to the Albanian shore where she would certainly have to be abandoned. In such a situation the fate of the surviving members of her crew would, at the least, be open to considerable doubt. The Admiral's second intention was that, if the *Saumarez*, by her own efforts and the help he was already planning, could remain seaworthy, the *Volage* should try to tow her to the nearest friendly anchorage—Corfu, the port they had left only ninety minutes earlier.

On receiving his instruction Commander Paul gave the order to increase speed, and the destroyer steamed down the centre of the swept corridor at eighteen knots. Admiral

Kinahan's next signal was to the *Leander*. He ordered Captain Otway-Ruthven to steam past the *Saumarez* but to make no attempt to assist. The Admiral reasoned that the smaller, more manoeuvrable *Volage* was best suited for the task of towing in the restricted waters of the swept channel. In addition, the smaller draught of the destroyer would make her less vulnerable in what was obviously an unknown and uncharted minefield. *Leander* was to carry on north through the channel, and then proceed at her best possible speed right round the island and return to the anchorage, ready to give whatever help she could —*if* the *Saumarez* managed to stay afloat, *if* the *Volage* managed to tow her back to harbour.

Captain Otway-Ruthven acknowledged his orders and down in the engine room the throttles were pushed on and on to send the old cruiser (she was laid down in 1930) surging through the water at a speed she had not touched since her last full power trials. The metal decks above the engine and boiler rooms showed her exertions; the heat could be felt even through the soles of shoes. As she swept past the *Saumarez*, lying bows down only half a mile away, the ratings lined her starboard side. Everyone felt the frustration of impotency and sympathy. A young seaman, aged nineteen, reflected the thoughts of many when he said, 'Christ, that could have been us.' Another rating, realizing that the deeper-draughted cruiser was nearing the spot where *Saumarez* had struck a mine, replied, 'Yes, mate—and it still could.'

The author was closed up at his Action Station in a radar office aboard *Leander* as the cruiser steamed past the *Saumarez*. I remember thinking, as we slipped out of Corfu Harbour and headed north, that it was slightly ludicrous to be operating a radar set designed to give a warning of the approach of enemy aircraft when Albania could not even boast of an air force. But orders are orders in any Service and are designed to meet any eventuality. The first I knew of the disaster was a hammering on the water-tight door of the radar office on the upper deck, which was shut in accordance with damage control regulations, and in order to keep the office dark so that the luminous radar picture could be seen more clearly.

Outside a shipmate shouted, 'Come out and look! It's the *Saumarez*; she's been hit by something and she's on fire. It looks as though she's going down.' I unfastened the heavy clips of the door and stepped out, blinking after the darkness of the radar office. The destroyer was immediately on our starboard beam. The black smoke streamed away from her bows like a long, chiffon scarf being ruffled by the wind. Men could be seen darting in and out of the smoke as they tried to get to the seat of the fire. Someone said quietly, 'It doesn't seem *right*, somehow.' It was a strange word for anyone to use in the circumstances, but most people knew what the man meant. He was trying to express the feeling shared by everyone that a thing like this just should *not* happen in peacetime.

Some of the men standing on *Leander's* upper deck as the cruiser swept by had friends aboard the *Saumarez*. One young sailor, just out of his teens, said quietly, 'God, I wonder if Sharkey's all right. We had a run ashore together only last night. I got a bit sloshed and I don't think I could have got back to the quayside without him.' It was a silly, inconsequential detail to mention at a time like that; but those are the times when you remember little human details which add up to friendships.

Someone said, 'I wonder if it really was a mine?' He got a reply which showed a simple logic. 'Of course it was a mine, because if it had been the guns we would all be firing back now, wouldn't we? The skipper said we would, didn't he?'

'I wish it had been the guns,' said another rating. 'Then we could be firing back; not just standing here looking and doing nothing.' And then came that word again as he added, 'It doesn't seem *right*, somehow.'

Another man spoke. 'She's drifting towards the shore. You can tell from the way the wind's blowing the smoke. What the hell will happen if she runs aground there? After all, the Albanians don't like us, do they?' Was ever a truth more logically achieved, more simply expressed!

Admiral Kinahan, his binoculars continually trained on the blazing, drifting *Saumarez*, was also concerned about that very problem. The destroyer was now perilously close to drifting out of the swept channel and into a known minefield off the Albanian coast. Her position was growing more desperate. Admiral Kinahan knew that she would never be able to withstand the effect of another mine, if, indeed, she was going to survive the damage from the one which had already crippled her.

Aboard the *Volage*, now closing in at eighteen knots, Commander Paul spoke to the crew over the ship's broadcasting system. He told them exactly what they were going to try to do and he was perfectly frank about the danger involved. *Saumarez*, he said, was drifting close to a known minefield. They would probably have to manoeuvre inside the minefield in order to get the flotilla leader in tow. And never far from everyone's mind was the thought, 'What will the shore batteries do? How will they react?'

Now that they had a Royal Navy vessel lying crippled right under their barrels, would the Albanians be able to resist the temptation further to reinforce their claim to the right to control which ships used the Corfu Channel and to give further evidence of their will to back their claim with force?

As *Volage* drew close to the *Saumarez* parties of seamen on her quarter deck prepared the towing wires. Capstans were tested and heaving lines coiled and laid ready on the deck. Watchers on the upper decks of the *Leander* got their last view of the *Saumarez* as the cruiser turned to port and steered on her new course for the sixty-mile, full-circle dash round the island of Corfu. As the intervening northern tip of Corfu island finally cut off the view of the stricken destroyer, one young rating, not yet old enough to draw his daily tot of rum,* said, 'Poor bastards. Wonder if we'll ever see 'em again? And there's blokes on her just waiting for their demob numbers to come up.'

Further announcements and orders from the bridge of

* It was drawn at the age of twenty, but has now been discontinued.

55

Leander ended thoughts like these. There was vital work to be done so that the cruiser would be able to give the most effective help to the *Saumarez* and her wounded men. Portable fire-fighting equipment was broken out from the stores and tested. Medical supplies—bandages, anti-burn lotions, penicillin and morphine—were prepared. The medical officers packed their bags ready to go aboard *Saumarez*. Camp beds, which some men slept in rather than hammocks, were gathered together for the use of the wounded, or for men who would have lost everything when the forward messdecks went up in flames.

Captain Selby had already signalled to Admiral Kinahan that he had confirmed by early checks on the area of the explosion that there had been many casualties, both dead and injured, and he feared the list might grow even higher, for he suspected (rightly, as it turned out) that some men had literally vanished in the explosion. In addition large areas of the ship forward of the bridge, from the keel to the upper deck, were now either in the grip of the fires or cut off by them. He knew that there were almost certainly men trapped in the fire area—he was to refer to that part of the ship in his subsequent report to the Admiralty as a 'raging inferno'—beyond any hope of rescue.

By now *Volage* had approached to within a few hundred feet of the *Saumarez*. Commander Paul, leaning over the wing of his bridge, ordered reduced revolutions from the engine room and the destroyer eased up slowly towards her flotilla leader as he considered the best way to get her in tow. The situation was difficult for the *Volage* and, by now, critical for the *Saumarez*. Any attempt to get a tow-line aboard the *Saumarez* would be hampered by the black smoke gushing from the internal fires, and by the huge patches of blazing oil on the sea around her.

A new and growing hazard was the depth of the water into which *Saumarez* was drifting. Both ships were getting uncomfortably close to a dangerous shoal area off Saranda, where the depth of the sea was only twelve feet—shallow enough to ground the *Saumarez*, with her bows sagging under the weight of water. Another worrying factor was that the shoals which shift with the currents could not be guaranteed to appear accurately on the navigation chart.

Commander Paul eased his destroyer under the stern of *Saumarez*, carefully choosing an area which was free of blazing oil on the sea. Heaving lines snaked across the few yards of water separating the two destroyers, a tow rope was passed and secured, and *Volage* was ready to tow *Saumarez*, stern first, away from the shoals and out to sea again.

Suddenly officers on the bridge of *Volage* stiffened. There, aboard *Saumarez*, they saw a man appear from somewhere between decks with a piece of blazing cotton waste in his hand and dash towards the ship's side with the clear intention of throwing it overboard as quickly as he could. The ships were still in seas covered with unignited fuel oil; it needed only a flame to set whole new areas of the sea ablaze. On *Volage* Lieut Hicks Beach reacted instinctively. He shouted, 'No! Don't throw it! Oil on the water!' Other officers and men took up the cry. 'We screamed and screamed at him,' another man recalled, 'But he didn't seem to hear us. Or he didn't *want* to hear us.'

As the watchers from *Volage* looked helplessly on, the man flung the piece of cotton waste and it fell in a gentle parabola of flames and tiny sparks on to the surface of the sea. Immediately one of the perils from which *Volage* was about to tow *Saumarez* was visited on the battered destroyer again. The flames spread along the patches of oil, darting from wave top to wave top, running in little rivulets of fire down the sides of waves to link up separate patches of oil into a completed carpet of flame, menacing both destroyers. What happened next is not entirely clear in every detail. Men who were there find it difficult, in view of the hectic circumstances and passage of time, to recall accurately. Commander Paul, in his official report on the incident, written the following day, refers to a 'misunderstanding' between the two ships. The relevant passage in this report says:

I passed close to her stern, and passed lines with the intention of towing her to seaward stern first, but an oil fire developed on the water off her starboard side which forced me to increase the distance to some extent and, in the course of subsequent misunderstanding between the quarter decks, the end of the manilla (the tow rope) was lost.

Another theory is that, anxious to tow *Saumarez* away from all her dangers as quickly as possible, Commander Paul took the strain on the tow line before sufficient rope had been passed between the two ships and it parted as it tautened. Whatever the reason, the tow was lost and *Saumarez* was again drifting helplessly on to a lee shore under the barrels of hostile guns. Already so much had happened; so many men had been killed or wounded. Yet, at this moment, only seventeen minutes had passed since *Saumarez* hit the mine. It was 3.10 p.m. as Commander Paul, one eye on the drifting destroyer and one eye on the chart showing the threatening shoal water, made a tight turn to starboard and carefully approached *Saumarez* again from the opposite direction. For the second time the difficult manoeuvre of passing the towline was attempted. Black smoke from *Saumarez* and from the blazing oil on the sea, swirled around the bridge and the quarter deck party on the stern trying to pass the tow. *Saumarez* at one stage seemed to be capable of giving herself, and her rescuer, some assistance. Down in the engine room and the Number Two boiler room, the stokers and engineer officers had managed to raise a little steam. It heartened everyone when it was seen that *Saumarez* could move herself, however slowly. But just as quickly as hopes were raised so were they dashed. After a few seconds the engines spluttered and died. They would never turn again.

Commander Paul manoeuvred *Volage* to get his stern against the stern of *Saumarez* once again and the two crews were able to start handling the 150 feet of tow rope and securing it ready for *Volage* to take the strain. During this operation, made extremely difficult by the confined waters, the smoke from the fires and the wallowing of the helpless destroyer, *Volage* received a gash in her bows. As she drifted slowly past *Saumarez* to allow the tow to be passed, the ships got too close and one of the metal stanchions supporting the quarter deck awning sliced through the bows of *Volage*. The damage was by no means serious, just a gash in the plates well above the water-line which any dockyard could repair in a couple of days. But a decision about that damage would, exactly forty-six minutes later, cost the lives of eight more men.

It was now 3.30 p.m., thirty-seven minutes since *Saumarez* struck the mine. Commander Paul was ready to start towing the destroyer back into the swept channel. But they were to be delayed yet again, this time by one of the most bizarre moments of the whole incident. A small wooden boat, rather like a fishing coble, was seen approaching the two destroyers from the direction of Saranda Bay. The coxswain steered it straight for the *Volage* and, as it drew nearer, watchers on the two destroyers could see that it was carrying a white flag and the Albanian flag with the emblem of the double eagle. Commander Paul's account of the incident in his official report is brisk and sailorlike and completely unemotional.

> A motor launch, heavily armed with small arms, approached. A man describing himself as the Harbour Master made the following remarks in Italian:
> 'I know nothing of your coming here.
> 'What are you doing here?
> 'Where do you come from?'
> I answered that a reply to his question would be communicated later.

What actually happened was that Commander Paul ordered his First Lieutenant, David Scott,* to investigate. The young officer took with him as interpreter a Maltese steward, one of the wardroom staff, who spoke Italian. He went down to the starboard waist, where the boat had pulled alongside the

---

* Now Rear-Admiral David Scott, Commander, British Naval Staff, Washington.

destroyer, and the conversation (of which Commander Paul gave a very brief and very much edited précis in his official report) took place.

Lieut Scott could see a number of men aboard the boat. One man kept a machine-gun trained on him throughout the conversation. The Harbour Master, if indeed the visitor was such, made no attempt to offer any assistance to the *Volage* or her crippled flotilla leader. No inquiries were made about the dead or wounded. No help from the shore in fighting the fires aboard *Saumarez* was offered. According to Commander Paul's report of the incident, the Harbour Master was told that 'a reply to his questions would be communicated later'. It was a strictly accurate, if somewhat euphemistic, phrase. In fact the Harbour Master was told to shove off in terms which naval officers do not use except under extreme provocation. As the boat turned and headed back towards Saranda (covered by an Oerlikon gun which had been trained on it throughout the incident) Commander Paul returned to the problem of towing *Saumarez* away.

Aboard *Mauritius*, still standing guard over the two destroyers two miles away, Admiral Kinahan, after hurried consultations with senior officers, began to summon the full available resources of the Mediterranean Fleet. The light fleet carrier H.M.S. *Ocean* was still steaming out at sea for a rendezvous with the two cruisers and destroyers which now would never be made. The Commanding Officer of the *Ocean*, Captain Caspar John,* was ordered to recall the aircraft which had been airborne for spotting duties and to steam to Corfu Harbour. In the meantime H.M.S. *Raider*, the destroyer acting as escort to the aircraft carrier, was to steam at full speeed to the immediate assistance of the *Saumarez*. The time was now 3.38 p.m., forty-five minutes after the *Saumarez* had been mined. A few minutes later Captain John reported that all his aircraft had landed and he was heading for Corfu at twenty-two knots.

Of all the big ships in the Mediterranean Fleet in the

* Later First Sea Lord.

immediate area, *Ocean* was the one which *Saumarez* needed most. She had fire fighting crews, specially trained to tackle fierce blazes on ships at sea, and all the latest equipment, including foam apparatus. *Saumarez* was in desperate need of such help. Her fire main gone, her auxiliary fire-fighting pumps lost in the blast or isolated by the blaze, she could rely only on a few hand pumps and auxiliary pumps sent over from *Mauritius* in a motor-boat. The destroyer also desperately needed the help of *Ocean's* fully-equipped hospital and its staff of doctors and sick berth attendants.

Men who had been trapped below decks were still emerging on to the upper deck where officers questioned them urgently. 'Any more trapped down there? Did you see anyone? Did you hear anyone?'

It was when men answered that third question that the most horrific facet of *Saumarez's* agony began to emerge—the fate of the men in the wireless office and the transmitting station. These two compartments were in the heart of the ship, just forward of the point where the mine hit, and in the main damage area around the canteen passageway. The wireless office was, of course, staffed with radio operators sending and receiving messages between the ships. Men, trained to put secret messages into code, or decypher incoming information, were also on watch in the office.

The transmitting station in any warship is the nerve centre of its fighting efficiency, controlling, as it does, the firing of the ship's main armament. Both these vital compartments are invariably close to the ship's bridge for ease of communication. And, while no part of a warship can ever be termed 'safe' during violent action, the wireless office and the transmitting station, sited in the centre of the ship, could be reckoned to be less likely to be 'knocked out' by mines or torpedoes than other positions. It became a theory with little meaning for the men on watch in those two compartments. There were believed to be about sixteen of them; the reason for the doubt will soon be painfully clear. The wireless office and transmitting station were only twenty feet above, and slightly forward of, the point of impact of the mine. The force of the explosion, bursting through the heart of the destroyer, turned the area immediately above the blast into a mass of twisted metal. Solid steel floors were rippled and concertinaed until they resembled switchback railways.

The wireless office and the transmitting station were the only upper deck compartments in the immediate area which were manned for Action Stations; unoccupied compartments close at hand ironically escaped with relatively minor damage. The T.S. and the W.T. offices became steel prisons and, eventually, steel coffins.

The force of the blast jammed the doors. Inside the compartments pieces of heavy electrical equipment torn from their mountings fell across doorways. No one could get in to save the men. They could not, by themselves, get out. What exactly happened inside those two compartments will never be known, for not one man survived. One can only reconstruct a picture from the evidence of experienced seamen aboard the *Saumarez*, many of whom had been blown up (some two or three times during the war) and from the reports of men who managed to escape before the passageway outside the two compartments was engulfed by the fire. One such was a stoker who was in the canteen passageway at the time of the explosion and, miraculously, survived. His laconic account of the incident as it affected him hides the considerable danger from which he and his mates escaped. And, no doubt deliberately, it dwells only briefly on the fate of the men in the wireless and transmitting compartments.

When we hit the mine a sheet of flame came up the hatchway from the lower messdeck. My hair was singed and my back slightly burned. I ran into the port passageway and the door jammed behind me. All the bathroom bulkheads had caved in and the only light was from an Oldham secondary lamp welded to a bulkhead. There were five of us together and another leading stoker tried to wrench this lamp off. He succeeded at the second attempt. He passed the lamp to a leading seaman, who told us to catch hold of one another and he led us out on to the upper deck. In doing this I cut my right leg climbing over some debris; I was wearing only my white tropical shorts. While I was in the passageway I heard the seamen in the transmitting station and the telegraphists in the wireless room screaming, as they were trapped.

One man who *should* have been at Action Stations in the wireless office owes his life to the fact that he was tired. With two other telegraphists he had been on watch the previous night, and they were resting on their messdeck when the call to Action Stations was sounded. This man, Mr Roy Lewis, now living in Canada, remembers:

The chief telegraphist told us all to report to the main wireless office. We griped about this as we were trying to catch up on our sleep, and the main wireless office was overstaffed anyway. It seemed pointless and it appeared the chief agreed, because he gave us the alternative of manning the emergency wireless office back aft, or staying on the messdeck—as long as we kept out of sight. One of us, we knew him as Nobby Hall, decided to stay on the messdeck, and myself and the other telegraphist went to the emergency office.

About an hour later there was a tremendous thump and we looked at each other, trying to guess what had happened. We tried to contact the main wireless office on the telephone but there was no answer. There was no answer either when we tried to contact the bridge. We left the office to investigate and saw lots of other blokes all making their way to the upper deck, asking 'What's happened?' Up on deck I saw a sickening bulge on the starboard side. Fuel oil was escaping rapidly. Several of us ran towards the bridge to give what help we could. Fire had already broken out in compartments under the bridge and the desperately tragic part of it was that we could do nothing for the men trapped. I will never forget the screams of those men.

One of the trapped men, Lewis was later to learn, was Nobby Hall. It seems he had second thoughts about staying on the messdeck and had gone to his Action Station in the main wireless office. He died with the other men in the office.

A man who was in the heart of the explosion area but survived recalls:

> With another electrician I was up in the forward section of the ship checking the emergency water supplies in the stokers' messdeck. Suddenly there was a great flash and a bang and the compartment filled with smoke. I shouted out to my mate: 'We've been hit.' All the lights had gone out. We found the ladder to the passageway above by the light of an emergency lamp which glimmered for a while on the ladder. When we got into the passageway we tried to go aft, away from the danger area, but we found that the bulkhead of the transmitting station had bulged right out, blocking our way along the passage. We then felt our way forward in the darkness. I realized my left arm was painful and my head, too. We found another ladder leading upwards. Daylight showed for a moment and we got up into what had been the petty officers' mess. It was a shambles. We got out on to the upper deck behind 'A' gun turret. By now the ship was listing badly; it seemed as though she was split in two. I went to the sick bay about the pain in my hand and my head. They put some purple ointment on and said I had been burned. It was the first time I realized it.

A further account of what was happening in the area of the transmitting station and the wireless office comes from a radar operator. He was only thirty feet away from the explosion. He received multiple injuries and severe burns in the blast and spent two years in hospital.

As the surface radar sets were not operating, because we were so close to land, I was sitting in a doorway of the radar office when the mine struck. I was talking to a forward damage control party standing in the passage when the explosion occurred. I never saw any of the damage control party again and I think they were all killed. I was blown out of the doorway and landed on the escape hatch from Number One boiler room, which opened up underneath me with flames shooting out through the hatch.

Instinct made me close the hatch, but the flames caught me in the face and blinded me for about a month. My hands, face and legs were also severely burned. I had a vision of everything going around like a whirlwind and in the flash I could see bodies flying around. Then I couldn't see anything. I was blinded. But I knew I had only two yards to make it to the open deck and I remembered the drill I had been taught in Devonport Barracks about what to do if you are trapped in a smoke-filled room, and I began to feel my way out. I put my hands against the bulkhead and couldn't feel a thing, possibly because my hands were so badly burned. I kept on walking—but I was walking the wrong way. I apparently went in towards where the mine had struck and then I passed out. Luckily for me I had been unable to climb over the decks which had been buckled by the explosion, and it was here that a rescue party found me and got me out to safety.

If I had managed to stumble any farther they might never have found me. They told me later that the men in the transmitting station had no chance, although one man had a miraculous escape. The blast blew open a door in the transmitting room and a seaman was sucked out by the draught and thrown against a bulkhead. Then the door crashed closed again and the remainder of the men were trapped. They said the gun crews who were linked up to the transmitting station by direct telephone lines could hear the lads screaming.

The end for the men in the transmitting station and wireless room came with the advancing flames. Mercifully it did not take as long as does the telling of it here. The two compartments could not be opened, until the following morning, when the fires were out and the blackened, twisted metal which had once been the heart of the ship had cooled sufficiently to allow inspection parties to go below the upper deck. It was a grim sight. The men were unrecognizable. Members of the inspection team who had fought throughout the war and were no strangers to violent death, turned away. Many were close to tears. Because of the obvious difficulties of positive identification the men in these two compartments are still officially listed in Admiralty records as 'missing, presumed killed'.

By now *Volage* had taken the strain on the towing line and *Saumarez*, still blazing fiercely, began to move away slowly towards the swept channel. The tow was made extremely difficult by the fact that the bows of *Saumarez*, sagging in the water, caused the destroyer to veer wildly from side to side. That this slow, lashing action while passing through a minefield exposed them to the added risk of hitting another mine, was not lost on the *Saumarez* survivors.

In the main damage area the fires still burned fiercely. From the moment the fire main failed soon after the explosion the fires had raged virtually out of control. The portable pumps sent over from *Mauritius* were able only to contain the fire. There was no question of their being able to extinguish it, not even with the puny yet unremitting help which teams of men gave with the available hand pumps. One man who worked with these teams on the hand pumps remembers, 'We pumped until we dropped—literally. Then we had a rest and went back for another bash. Well, there wasn't much else to do, was there?'

Another man, working a hand pump, looked down at the sea lapping only two feet below him and remarked to a companion, 'I wonder how many more mines there are down there.'

Admiral Willis, the Mediterranean C-in-C, was sailing from Piraeus, the port of Athens, to Argostoli in his flagship, the cruiser H.M.S. *Liverpool*, when he was informed of the disaster. He had left port only a couple of hours earlier on what he expected to be a very pleasant ending to the Fleet's autumn cruise—the regatta. He had as his guest aboard the *Liverpool* the Greek Navy Minister, a courteous reciprocal gesture from a Fleet which had spent pleasant weeks in Greek waters. This idyll was now shattered and the *Liverpool* increased to full speed on a new course—direct to Corfu. The news, and there was worse to come, had horrified the Admiral. He had been personally involved at the highest levels of the Admiralty in organizing Britain's show of force through the Corfu Channel. He is now living in retirement at Petersfield, in Hampshire, and it was there that he recalled:

> My first reaction on hearing the news was one of absolute incredulity—that a terrible thing like this should happen in peacetime. But it was something which no one could have foreseen.

But was it? During the researches for this book a number of men who were involved in the incident have expressed their own incredulity that no one at the Admiralty foresaw the possibility that Albania might protect her disputed waters with mines. It would be unfair merely to dismiss this view as one of being wise after the event. Albania had made her intentions to defend her shores abundantly clear in the belligerent speeches by Enver Hoxha *and* by the shelling of the *Orion* and the *Superb*. Yet, as has been noted, the cruisers had not taken the precaution of streaming paravanes, which was one active measure against mines which the ships of the force could have taken. Was this failure to assess Albania's intentions an act bordering on criminal negligence, or was it just one more example of the British Government's inability to take Hoxha and his comrades seriously? On the question of the mines, Admiral Willis put his views forcefully.

> I knew of no reason at the time, nor have I thought of one since, why anyone should have suspected that the Albanians would lay mines, or have mines laid for them.

Such a possibility never occurred to me or, as far as I can recall, to anyone at the Admiralty. Why should it? Civilized nations just do not lay mines in peacetime and keep them a secret.

The whole appalling business upset me deeply, especially as so many of the casualties were just youngsters. But I am afraid that incidents such as this are the price the British Navy has always paid for maintaining the freedom of the seas for everybody else.

On board *Volage*, Commander Paul was only a few minutes from paying his price for the security of the seas. With *Saumarez* now being towed slowly towards safety Commander Paul turned his mind to another problem—the damage to the starboard bow of his ship. He ordered the forward damage control party to make temporary repairs to the gash, which was eight feet long and one foot wide. It was twelve feet above the sea level. The damage control party consisted of six men—an engine room artificer, a stoker petty officer, a leading stoker and three stokers. They were led by a young engineering officer who had joined the ship in Corfu only three days previously, Sub-Lieut H. G. Price, of the R.N.V.R. The *Volage* was his first ship; he was nineteen years of age.

They entered the forward messdeck and began to carry out their temporary repair by packing the gash with any 'padding' they could find. They used a lashed-up hammock, cushions from the messdeck seats, any spare clothing left lying around. Then quick drying cement was plastered over the padding. At intervals the Engineer Officer, Lieut S. A. Nash* a destroyer

* Nash, now living in retirement at Lee-on-Solent, had a remarkable career spanning no less than fifty-three years. He joined the Navy in 1916 as an artificer apprentice. As an engine room artificer he served in battleships, cruisers and destroyers and, in 1929, was commissioned as an engineering officer. During the 1939–45 war he served on destroyers operating in the Mediterranean on Malta convoys and taking part in the landings in North Africa. He was mentioned in despatches three times. After eleven years of continuous service as a chief engineer he was appointed station engineer at the Royal Naval Air Station at Gosport in 1950; he retired in 1955. He then joined the Royal Navy Scientific Service and made a valuable contribution to the development of the steam catapult for launching planes from aircraft carriers. He finally retired in 1970.

man of vast experience (and at forty-five years of age old enough to be the young sub-lieutenant's father) made periodic inspections of the work. On the forecastle above them two petty officers were standing by to operate the capstan. They had been ordered there by Commander Paul when he thought he might have to drop anchor to save his ship and *Saumarez* from going aground in the shallow water. They were still there, even though *Volage* was now heading steadily for the swept channel.

At 4.0 p.m. Lieut Nash made his last inspection of the repair work on the damaged bows. Sub-Lieut Price's party had almost finished the job. Planks of wood had been put against the packing and they were shoring up the planks with thick timber to give it extra strength. Nash returned to the bridge and reported to Commander Paul that satisfactory progress was being made. He recalled later: 'I was anxious for them to finish the job and get out of it. I was never happy about their being in the bows when we were passing through a minefield.'

At about 4.15 p.m. Sub-Lieut Price sent one of his young stokers away in response to a request for assistance aft. A few seconds later disaster struck again. For the second time within eighty-two minutes the sound of a massive explosion reverberated around the Albanian hills. The *Volage* reared into the air like a startled horse. Men on the upper deck of the *Saumarez*, still fully occupied fighting the fire, swung round towards the noise. They saw a huge water-spout shooting up above the bows of the *Volage*. The tow rope slackened and flopped into the sea as the *Volage* lost speed. As she swung round in the wind, men stared with incredulity on their faces— the whole of the bows of the *Volage* had vanished. She, too, had struck a mine. She had hit it exactly head on. In a split second forty feet of the destroyer, from the fore peak to just in front of 'A' gun turret, had vanished. Messdecks, store rooms, the paint shop, the cable locker containing tons of anchor cable, the anchors themselves, literally dissolved in the air. Seamen on the quarter deck keeping watch on the tow-line felt the blast rippling through the decks beneath their feet. The blast was transmitted through the sea separating the two destroyers and felt aboard *Saumarez*.

Capain Selby, still at his emergency conning position behind the funnel of the *Saumarez*, saw a huge spout of water shoot up to the height of the *Volage* mast—seventy-two feet—and pieces of wreckage from the bows flung even higher than that.

Lieut Shackleton saw the explosion, too. He had just come up from the engine room for some fresh air when *Volage* hit the mine. He immediately asked for, and was granted, permission to evacuate all personnel from the engine room and Number Two boiler room. It seemed to him there was no point in risking men down below while his engines were useless and the destroyer was obviously in a minefield. The stokers and engine room artificers thankfully trooped on to the upper deck and joined the men fighting the fires.

On the bridge of the *Volage* everyone was flung to the deck. Huge pieces of metal, some weighing up to half a ton, crashed on to the bridge, one piece narrowly missing Commander Paul. As the bridge personnel staggered to their feet, marvelling that no one had been injured, they saw an amazing sight. The mast behind them was festooned with articles of clothing which had been blown out of the forward messdecks and flung into the air on the water spout. Shirts, vests, underpants, seamen's blue collars, socks and towels were draped in crazy disarray on the radio and radar aerials, around the crows' nest look-out post, in the rigging, among the rungs of the ladder reaching up to the top of the mast, all flapping gently in the wind. Lieut Hicks Beach remembers it as 'a very strange sight indeed. It was like some zany, mixed-up washing line.'

Commander Paul's first thought was for the men of the damage control party who, at the moment of the explosion, were still between decks in the bows of the ship. Lieut Hicks Beach raced down from the bridge and tried to get in to the forward messdeck, but twisted metal blocked his way. But young Sub-Lieut Price and his party were already beyond help. They were in the section of the bow which disintegrated. They were never seen again.

Petty Officer Joseph Knott, who was standing-by on the forecastle ready to drop anchor if necessary, was killed immediately. Stoker Petty Officer Cyril Keeton, who was on the forecastle in case the capstan was required, was blown against a bulkhead and had multiple injuries, including a severe head wound. Lieut Hicks Beach bound up his head with the only thing available at the time—a piece of a navigation chart which had been blown from the bridge. It was to no avail; Keeton died soon afterwards.

A seaman who had been on duty close to the forecastle was picked up by the blast and hurled 100 feet towards the stern. He staggered to his feet with a dazed 'How did I get here?' look on his face. He had severe injuries but he survived. And then, as the ship's company began to shake themselves together in the first few seconds after the explosion, men on the upper deck were startled, to say the least, by the sight of a rating running the length of the ship from just aft of the shattered bows right to the quarter deck, shouting and screaming as though he were pursued by a devil. He was naked except for a pair of blue socks. When he reached the quarter deck he stopped, came to his senses and looked rather sheepish. At first it was thought that the unfortunate man had been caught in the blast of the explosion and had all his clothes stripped from his body. The truth turned out to be less dramatic. He had apparently been having a quiet and illegal 'kip' in a messdeck close to the explosion and the rearing of the forward end of the ship woke him up. Was ever a sleeper more rudely awakened! But retribution awaited; he was subsequently punished by loss of shore leave for being absent from his place of duty.

Another man whose first thoughts after the explosion went to the damage control party was Stoker Stanley Goodman, nineteen years of age—the man who, only seconds before, had been sent away from the bows. Many years later he recalled his impressions at the time.

My mates were blown to bits almost before my eyes. It isn't a nice thing to think about. There was Joss and Mick and Burney and Taffy—you forget their real names but you remember their nicknames. When Sub-Lieut Price told me to go aft I turned and went through the doorway in a bulkhead, when there was this almighty explosion, and that was that. There was just nothing left of the bow section where I had been; it was just a gaping hole. I missed death by half a minute or so.

As it was I was blown head first against a bulkhead and I had head injuries and a broken nose. When I got back to Devonport Barracks with some of the other wounded they discovered my head injury was a fractured skull. When I came out of hospital I visited Sub-Lieut Price's parents at their home in Newquay. He was listed as 'Missing, Presumed Killed'. I told them that he and the chaps with him stood no chance. They were very grateful to know the truth because, up to then his mother was still holding out hope, but his father seemed to know what I knew; that there was no chance at all.

Twenty-six years later Sub-Lieut Price and his seven shipmates—like the men who perished in the transmitting station and the wireless room aboard the *Saumarez*—are still listed in Admiralty records as "Missing, Presumed Killed".

At this stage in the story of The Corfu Incident we may justifiably examine an aspect of the tragedy which survivors of the *Volage*—and others deeply involved in the events of that October afternoon—have found disturbing. The fact that Commander Paul is not alive to defend his decisions (he died some years after the incident) should not dissuade us from trying to analyse his reasons for them, although in fairness it must be pointed out that a board of inquiry into the whole of The Corfu Incident accepted his decision. The question which many people ask is this: Why, when he knew that one destroyer had already hit a mine, and he was going to her aid in waters which probably contained other mines, did he have a damage control party between decks as far forward in the ship as it was possible to be?

The gash in the bow of the *Volage* was by no means serious. Unless the weather suddenly deteriorated, it was no threat to the safety or efficiency of his ship. Indeed, with the watertight doors closed immediately aft of the damaged compartment the destroyer would have been entirely sea-worthy in any foreseeable weather and sea conditions. Yet the damage repair party and the forecastle party were sent forward, with such tragic results.

It must be said immediately that the fact that he had ordered men into the bows of the ship in waters menaced by mines would not normally have given Commander Paul cause for concern. People who have no knowledge of naval matters naturally assume that if a ship moving through the water hits a moored mine the point of contact will be with the bows, and the damage will, therefore, invariably be in the forward part of the ship. I confess this was the view I held until I joined H.M.S. *Leander* and was allocated a place to sling my hammock which gave me great concern. It was right up in the bows of the cruiser—immediately aft of the paint store—in exactly the same relative position as that in which the *Volage* repair party was working when the bows disintegrated. I voiced my apprehensions to a long-serving sailor in a jocular way which, I hoped, hid my considerable unease.

'What about this, then? Right up in the eyes of the ship. Ah well, if we hit a mine I won't know much about it.'

The old sailor smiled and said, 'Don't worry yourself, sonny. You've got the safest berth in the ship.' He was, of course, quite right.

A ship moving at reasonable speed through the water pushes, by its own momentum, a considerable weight of water ahead of it. This water divides either side of the ship as the bow-wave, and then swings the mine away from the bow. It may, depending on varying factors, swing back on its cable and hit the ship amidships or astern, but very rarely does a moored mine explode on or under a ship's bows. There were two other factors which Commander Paul no doubt weighed in his mind before ordering the damage control party to repair the gash in the bows.

The first was the fact that *Volage*, towing the crippled *Saumarez*, was proceeding ahead only slowly. The small bow wave would not therefore afford its usual protection to the forward part of the ship.

Secondly, *Saumarez* with her water-logged bows swinging wildly, was not the easiest ship to tow. This swinging caused *Volage* herself to veer either side of her course, presenting a bigger surface of the forward part of the destroyer to any mines in the area. Commander Paul decided, as we have seen, to send the repair party to work. From his official report of the whole incident it is clear that he was extremely anxious to maintain the water-tight integrity of his ship. The thought of that gash in the bows obviously worried him. He was fully aware that the responsibility for getting *Saumarez* back to Corfu rested with him and him alone. It was a formidable load to bear. Any deterioration in the weather might make that gash —at present well above the water-line—a serious danger to his ship and the task it had to perform. But was it really worth risking the lives of the repair party and the forecastle crew over damage which Commander Paul describes in his own official report on the disaster as minor?

I put the question to Rear-Admiral Selby, now living in retirement in Wiltshire and devoting his energies to calmer waters in helping preserve the Kennet and Avon Canal. He thought long and deeply before he answered, fully aware that Commander Paul cannot now explain or defend his actions, if indeed they need to be defended. Finally he said:

> I don't think I would have taken that decision in the circumstance. The water-tight integrity of a ship is all-important, but one has to take into account all sorts of factors; in this case the factor was that the ship was in dangerous waters. I think I would have ordered the bulk-head immediately aft of the damaged compartment to

be shored up to give it extra strength, and then left the gashed bows to be repaired later. But officers, when they are new to the responsibilities of command, tend to react strictly 'according to the book'. That is what Reggie Paul did.

Immediately *Volage* struck the mine the tow line to the stern of *Saumarez* was slipped and officers rushed forward to check on the damage. The bow had been blown off square across the breadth of the ship, leaving what remained of the front end a tangled mass of jagged metal, pipes and trunking. However, the ship still had the things that *Saumarez* so cruelly lacked—steam and water. Steam had been switched on to the forecastle in case Commander Paul needed to drop anchor. The blast had broken the pipe and it now hissed from the shattered front section. Similarly, water which had been available in the fire-main encircling the ship, was now gushing from the ruptured main. The Engineering officer, Lieut Nash, was able to report to the bridge that the rest of the ship was entirely undamaged. Commander Paul picked up the radio microphone and contacted Admiral Kinahan in *Mauritius*, now out of sight behind a headland. And for the second time that afternoon Kinahan received the simple, dramatic message, 'I have been mined forward'. If there remained any thought in the Admiral's mind that the mining of *Saumarez* could have been an accident, the second explosion removed it entirely.

Back in London, when the news of the double disaster was received at the Admiralty, one can only assume that the reaction of their lordships was one of utter dismay. They had, on the instructions of the Government, laid on a show of force in an attempt to achieve political ends—a fair description of gun-boat diplomacy down the years.* Now the operation had

* In his book *Gunboat Diplomacy* (Chatto and Windus, for the Institute of Strategic Studies, 1971) James Cable includes The Corfu Incident in a list of incidents over the last fifty years which can be classed as gun-boat diplomacy. He defines this as 'the use or threat of limited naval force, otherwise than as an act of war, in order to secure advantage or to avert loss, either in the furtherance of an international dispute or else against foreign nationals within the territory or the jurisdiction of their own state'.

quite literally blown up in their faces. The Government had good reason to think that the Albanians most certainly had not 'learned to behave themselves'.

But Mr Atlee and his Cabinet, an administration born of a war-time Coalition and now dedicated to the propagation of peace, must have considered that the price paid for this knowledge was appallingly high. And even as the first reports of the disaster were being received in Whitehall, it was by no means certain that the full price had yet been extracted. With the tow from the *Volage* slipped, the helpless *Saumarez* was once more drifting in the minefield. *Volage*, too, was drifting with her as her officers checked on the damage. Clearly there were other mines in the immediate area. If either ship had struck the other it would almost certainly have sunk her, with further disastrous loss of life. In addition, everyone aboard the two destroyers was aware of the uncomfortable proximity of the Albanian shore batteries. Of all the harrowing moments of that day, and almost another twelve hours of it were still to be endured, this was the darkest hour.

Rear-Admiral Gueritz, First-Lieutenant at the time, recalls:

> Aboard the *Saumarez* we felt very, very lonely at that moment. There we were, drifting helplessly on to a lee shore. The *Volage* which, seconds ago, had been towing us to safety, was now herself badly damaged. We did not know whether she would be able to resume towing us. Our own fires were still raging and we were making no progress against them. There was the danger of our hitting another mine, or of running aground. Darkness was beginning to fall, and we could see no sign of *Leander* or *Mauritius*; they were both behind a headland. Yes, we felt very, very lonely.

Lonely indeed, and, perhaps, not a little bit afraid. Would anyone have been surprised if, confronted by these dangers and uncertainties, the faces of the scores of youngsters aboard the destroyers showed a trace of fear or even of panic. But they did not. Rear-Admiral Gueritz recalls only one incident aboard the *Saumarez* when a little apprehension broke the surface. A young stoker approached him and asked, in a carefully casual tone, 'Should I undo the lashings of the Carley floats, sir?' In a similarly casual, courteous voice he was thanked for the suggestion but told that it was not yet necessary to think of launching the life-saving equipment.

One man remembers:

> I was at the stern of the ship, having a breather from operating a hand pump, when the first lieutenant came up. He asked me if I was afraid, and he gave me some words of encouragement and suggested that I go back forward and help with the pumping. Until that time I don't recall being particularly frightened, but after that I was waiting all the time for the next explosion.

And Rear-Admiral Selby subsequently added this tribute to his crew. 'They proved themselves to be among the best I had ever commanded. I felt I would have sailed with them into anything.'

It was now 4.30 p.m., fourteen minutes after *Volage* had been mined. Commander Paul decided to move ahead slowly to try to take the *Saumarez* in tow again. But he had to abandon this plan when he heard what he described as 'sinister noises low down forward', and his ship took on a sudden list of seven degrees to port. Another inspection showed that the 'sinister noise' was the ripping and wrenching of metal as the remains of the shattered bows hanging beneath the surface tried to part company with the rest of the destroyer. Commander Paul was fearful that the list would become more pronounced; the ship had already lost some stability. To try to correct the list he ordered loose fittings on the port side to be thrown overboard. Ready-use ammunition from the forward 4.7 inch guns was heaved into the sea. The heavy stowage trolley for the destroyer's motor dinghy followed the shells over the side. Depth charges set to 'Safe' were rolled into the sea and the chief engineer began switching water and fuel oil from tanks on the port side to the starboard side. Two torpedoes, set to sink, were fired and one member of the *Volage* crew remembers this moment in particular. As a precaution, a lifeboat and the ship's motor boat had been lowered into the sea after the *Volage* hit the mine. They were lying off the ship when the torpedoes were fired and to one of the men in the lifeboat, Able Seaman George Swift, it looked 'as though our own captain was trying to finish us off'.

Further hurried attempts to correct the list by dumping heavy gear were abandoned when the chief engineer pointed out that firing torpedoes from the tubes towards the stern was not helping his attempts to correct the list. Far from losing weight at the stern, he needed *extra* weight there to compensate for the list forward. Commander Paul accepted this view and no more torpedoes were fired. Instead, at the suggestion of another officer, work began on moving the remaining torpedoes to the stern of the ship on the starboard side, to help counter-act the list. A sudden recurrence of the 'sinister noises low down forward' ended the need for any further attempts to correct the trim. With a grating and groaning of metal the remaining bow section finally broke away. That shattered section of *Volage* may be the final resting place of Sub-Lieut Price and the members of his damage control party. It lies more than 100 feet beneath the waves, so we will never know. There has never been any reason to try to recover what, in mercenary salvage terms, is no more than a few pounds worth of twisted hardware. And why, indeed, should anyone bother? A grave is a grave.

The departure of the remains of the bow section left the *Volage* floating on an even keel. Viewed from the stern she appeared to be completely undamaged. Her paintwork was unmarked, there were no signs of disarray on her upper decks. But up forward was a strange sight indeed. It was as if some monster hand wielding a huge axe had crudely chopped off forty feet of the bows at one stroke. Where a few minutes before had been a gracefully flared and pointed bow was now a grotesque, squared-off stump. The barrel of 'A' gun had caught the edge of the blast and had been forced upwards ten degrees out of normal elevation. 'B' gun turret immediately above and slightly astern, was undamaged and ready for action. Viewed from bow-on at sea level, as the crews of many small boats and the *Saumarez* throughout the long night to come were to see her, the remains of the forward part were a recognizable, if tangled, cross-section of the ship as it had been.

It was no doubt with considerable pride that Commander Paul was able to note in his report: 'Except that 'A' gun turret was put out of action and that steaming ahead was obviously drastically limited, fighting efficiency remained virtually unimpaired.'

Below the waterline what remained of the forward end of the keel was bent upwards like the front of a huge ski. But what was much more important to Commander Paul, the bulkhead immediately astern of the damage area, Number Thirty bulkhead, was intact and apparently seaworthy. Commander Paul, after some discussion with First Lieut Scott and Lieut Nash, decided it was feasible for him to attempt to rescue *Saumarez* once again by putting his shattered bows to her stern and towing her stern-first. For the third time that afternoon, he crossed into the minefield and eased his destroyer up to the stern of the *Saumarez*. As he approached an aldis lamp blinked an encouraging signal from Captain Selby, who could now see the extent of the damage to *Volage*'s bows, and who had been told of the casualties. It flashed: 'Hard luck, Reggie. Have another go. I think you can still tow me stern first.'

Saumarez was once again dangerously near the shoal water and, to save valuable time, a very short tow rope of thirty-six feet of four-inch wire was passed over her twisted forecastle and secured to bollards on the stern of the *Saumarez*. The engines of the *Volage* were put astern and, at a cautious two and a half knots both ships began moving stern first. The time was 5.0 p.m. Seventeen minutes later the two ships had reached the centre of the swept channel off Denta Point. *Volage* had crossed the minefield four times; for her the danger seemed to be over. But not for the *Saumarez*. The fires in the heart of the ship raged on, defying the efforts of her survivors to control them. As darkness fell, the plates on the ship's side and the upper deck above the fires glowed red-hot. It looked like a huge oven grill, and the plates hissed and spluttered as sea-water, and the intermittent showers which now began to fall, splashed on the glowing metal.

But, as ever, the spirit of the *Saumarez* crew was shown in flashes of humour. One young seaman, his uniform soaked in water and oil, his face blackened by the smoke, handed over his hose to a relief and cracked, 'I wish we had a few chestnuts. They would roast a treat on there.' Another man, looking in disgust at the comparative trickle of water coming from the hosepipe he was holding, suggested his fire-fighting efforts would be equally effective if he attended to the wants of nature.

In the starboard waist a seaman occupied his breather from fire-fighting duties in talking cheerily to the wounded and handing them lighted cigarettes. He himself had been burned about the arms and face but, after having the protective purple ointment painted on his burns, he had returned to duty. He handed a cigarette to a man whose head was swathed in bandages. 'Thanks very much,' he said. Then he smiled and added, 'Do you know, mate, that colour doesn't suit you!' As an aid to keeping up these spirits, Captain Selby ordered a special ration of rum all round.

On the bridge of the *Volage* Commander Paul and his officers were coping with the considerable problems of towing a ship stern-first while going stern first herself. The *Saumarez* was extremely sluggish and swung wildly from side to side on the short tow rope. Commander Paul decided to reinforce it with an eight-inch manilla rope. Another factor made life extremely difficult for the *Volage* bridge party. The wind, freshening slightly now, was coming from astern—actually over the bows. While this helped to maintain the towing speed it blew the fumes and smoke from the fires aboard *Saumarez* into their faces, stinging their noses and eyes. Tension heightened aboard *Volage* as she slowly approached the spot on the Albanian shore from where the machine gunner had fired earlier that afternoon. But, on this occasion, he kept quiet, 'somewhat to the disappointment of my pom-pom's crews', Commander Paul later recorded.

And so the two ships plodded on into the darkness. From the forward end of the *Volage* men watching over the towing wires marvelled that *Saumarez* remained afloat. The flames from her fires cast a flickering orange light over the sea; until the *Volage* electricians could pass emergency electric cables to her it was the only light she had. First Lieut Gueritz, one of the few officers who was not wounded, moved round the ship, directing the fire-fighting operations and giving words of encouragement to men who had been fighting the fires continuously for three hours. Two duties in particular which fell to Lieut Gueritz that afternoon were to stick in his mind. One was connected with the safety of a young seaman, who was believed trapped below in one of the messdecks. The other duty, strangely enough, concerned forty turkeys.

Gueritz had received a report that a man was trapped in the communication ratings' messdeck. There was, of course, no main lighting in the *Saumarez* and the messdeck was in complete darkness. By the light of his torch Gueritz peered down through the hatchway and he could see that the messdeck below was partly flooded. Nevertheless, he led two men down the hatchway and they lowered themselves into the water. It was up to their arm-pits as they half-waded and half swam through the compartment. It was an eerie experience. The water slopped around as the *Saumarez* wallowed in the troughs of the waves. Messdeck tables floated on the surface and bumped against the ship's plating. The explosion had blown rivets from the ship's side and, through the rivet holes, thin pencils of light pointed into the compartment like accusing fingers. The flotsam of disaster was on the oily water—a shoe or two, a seaman's cap, a clothes brush. And that was all. There was no sign of life—and having seen the state of the compartment, Gueritz expected none. But, if there was a body there, it was their duty to recover it for a decent burial.

This thought was in his mind when, wading slowly through the water, he put his foot on something soft and bulky. 'Oh, dear; we've found him,' he thought. Holding his torch aloft with one hand, Gueritz and the two seamen ducked beneath the water and pulled the object to the surface. No body—it was some man's lashed-up hammock, containing his mattress and blanket. The three men were happy to climb up the gangway and out of the blackness. 'The episode was rather unnerving,' Gueritz recalled. 'I am glad nothing like it has been repeated since.'

The incident concerning the turkeys was also a distressing one, but in a very different way. Before leaving Corfu harbour that afternoon, forty turkeys had been taken aboard and stowed in crates on the upper deck. They were scrawny birds, far removed from the plump specimens which we in Britain know. But, went the thinking, they *are* turkeys—and Christmas is not far away. It was intended that the cooks should pluck them and put them in the deep-freeze compartment, ready for the ship's Christmas dinner back in Malta. As it happened, the crew of the *Saumarez* would never see Christmas dinner aboard their ship in Malta. Those who were not killed were sent on survivor's leave and the *Saumarez* lay in Grand Harbour, Malta, with a small caretaker crew aboard as her future, or her final end, was decided. And the turkeys never graced a table in Malta or anywhere else.

When the *Saumarez* hit the mine the turkeys in their crates were flung into the air, and one or two of the crates burst open. Most of them had been drenched by the water-spout, and some had been charred by the fire blast. Gueritz decided that, even amidst the difficulties and dangers which overwhelmed the destroyer at that time, these wretched victims must be put out of their misery immediately. He called over Leading Steward Baldachino and together they wrung the necks of thirty-eight turkeys and threw them over the ship's side. Two turkeys which appeared to be unhurt escaped, but what happened to them is not definitely known. One was last seen being stalked by the ship's cat, and it is assumed that the cat at least had a turkey dinner. The other was found some days later right forward in the cable locker.   ·

It is an interesting facet of the story that, so long after The Corfu Incident, the moments which adhere most strongly to the memory are not the ones tinged with the dramatic, or even the horrific. The mind, healing its own wounds, draws a veil over such matters as the deaths of the men trapped in the wireless office and the transmitting station; of the cook, and his plaintive 'Help me, Help me'; or of the young sailor who pleaded for a bullet to release him from the agony of his burns. Instead, the memory gratefully seizes and stores away insignificant little cameos. For instance, the incident which impressed itself more firmly on the mind of Lieut Gueritz than a hundred others was having to put the turkeys out of their misery. Captain Selby remembers in particular two young men from his crew, men of vastly different backgrounds. One was a stoker, the son of a miner. The other was one of the Old Etonians in the ship's company, serving on the lower deck as a seaman.

Saumarez still had no electrical power. To pass his commands, and to call officers to the emergency bridge for reports on the situation, Captain Selby had a team of messengers, of which the Old Etonian was one. At the height of the battle to control the fires he turned to his captain and said, 'Sir, I am sure I could be much more use up forward helping to fight the fires than just running messages.' Captain Selby told him to 'double away smartly' to join the fire-fighting teams. Certainly he needed messengers, but his ship also needed the kind of spirit which the young man had shown.

The stoker had frequently confronted his captain—from the other side of the defaulters' table. From the moment he joined the ship he had been continually in trouble. Nothing really serious, just indiscretions like being late back from shore leave, late on parade, kit not up to standard. There was something rather pathetic about his attempts to cope with a naval career, brief and impermanent though it might be, and Selby found himself taking a special interest in the youngster and giving him an extra word or two of encouragement. Captain Selby never knew how the young chap got on in civilian life. But he wonders frequently, and the miner's son joins with the Old

Etonian in the captain's frequently remembered cameo.

At seven o'clock that evening surviving members of the *Saumarez* got the first real boost to their spirits. *Volage* managed to pass electric leads over her forward end and these were connected to the power terminals in the stern of the *Saumarez*. Now they had the comfort of light in their darkness. One man recalls, 'No one who wasn't there at the time can imagine what a boost those lights gave us. Somehow the darkness was associated in our minds with all the terrible things that had happened that day; the lights helped us to forget them for a little while.'

The power also gave them a boost in the form of cups of tea and soup. But more important it meant that a more powerful pump could now be used to supplement the hand pumps and the portable pumps from the *Mauritius*. And it gave a moment's rest to the men who had been manning the hand pumps in relays for more than four hours and were at the point of exhaustion. But the bigger pump could not be expected to do more than help contain the flames. As the two ships wallowed their way towards Corfu, their rate of progress about half normal walking pace, the plates of the *Saumarez* still glowed red in the night. Every now and then gutted compartments below decks collapsed and darting tongues of flame outlined the ship in ruddy silhouette and sent showers of sparks shooting into the sky. For no one was there any rest or respite. The only members of the crew not on their feet were the wounded, lying on the upper deck beneath the awnings and canvas screens which had been erected to give them some protection from the wind and rain. Some of those less seriously hurt had to be physically restrained from joining their shipmates fighting the fires.

But relief for the agony of the two ships was now getting near. The destroyer *Raider* was only a few miles away and was steaming fast through the southern approach to the channel. The aircraft carrier *Ocean* was on her way and the *Leander* had by now almost completed her dash round the island back to Corfu harbour. Admiral Willis, steaming at full speed for

Corfu, ordered the fleet hospital ship *Maine* to Corfu harbour to be ready to receive the wounded. But it was still by no means certain that both ships would make it to harbour, and evidence of this was seen in the presence of one man on what remained of the forecastle of the *Volage* and another on the stern of the *Saumarez*. Each man held an axe, ready to hack through the tow lines in the event of *Saumarez* foundering and imperilling *Volage*.

At 8.0 p.m. the ships passed Barchetta Rock, which marks the entrance to the narrowest part of the North Channel, and entered calmer waters. It was just five and a half hours since they had passed the rock heading in the opposite direction. Over his radio telephone Commander Paul received regular reports on the progress of the ships steaming to their aid, and he passed the information on to Captain Selby, whose radio communications were still out of action.

Aboard the *Ocean* the powerful fire-fighting equipment the *Saumarez* so desperately needed was being made ready. Crews specially trained to deal with fires at sea were being mustered by their equipment. In the *Ocean* sick bays, beds were prepared, for the aircraft carrier would arrive at Corfu before the *Maine* and the wounded desperately needing hospital treatment were to be transferred there. But, as the carrier ploughed on through the night towards Corfu and her mission of mercy, many officers and men aboard her found it difficult to believe that disasters such as this really occur in peacetime. It was the same feeling of unreality which observers aboard the *Mauritius* and *Leader* felt when they saw the *Saumarez* mined. At any rate, the evening routine in the aircraft carrier's wardroom was in no way disturbed—the officers dined in full mess kit as usual.

At 8.30 p.m. the crews of the *Volage* and the *Saumarez* saw the navigation lights and the mast-head light of a vessel approaching them at speed from the direction of Corfu harbour. It was the destroyer *Raider*. From the upper decks of the *Saumarez* came a ragged little cheer. Even some of the wounded, who had borne all the discomforts of lying on the upper deck for five and a half hours in addition to the pain from their wounds, managed a wan smile or the wave of a hand. Corfu Harbour was dead ahead and only five miles away; it seemed they would make it after all.

The original instruction to *Raider* when she was ordered to the Corfu Channel was to stand by in case *Volage* was unable to tow *Saumarez*. In addition, she was to be ready to protect the two destroyers if the Albanian coastal gunners opened up on them. Now, as *Raider* steamed slowly past the two ships and her captain assessed the situation, it seemed clear that *Volage* was quite capable of towing *Saumarez* into harbour. What Captain Selby needed most of all at this moment was additional help in fighting his fires and he ordered *Raider* close alongside to hose water on his red-hot plates to try to cool the ship down and let his own fire-fighting parties get closer to the seat of the blaze.

Through a loud-hailer Selby told *Raider's* captain to direct the hoses on to parts of the ship's sides which were reasonably intact and not into the section opened up by the explosion. His ship had already taken an immense amount of water in her shattered forward section, and there was a danger of her capsizing. In addition the weight of the water was dragging the forward section deeper and deeper into the sea. It was like a huge anchor hanging in the water and had cut *Volage's* towing speed to one knot—barely headway.

Raider closed to within fifty feet of *Saumarez* and for three hours her captain, with a touch of the engines here and there, kept her in position while the hoses sprayed the destroyer.

At 9.0 p.m. the crews of *Saumarez* and *Volage* saw their second encouraging sight in thirty minutes. At first it looked like dozens of glow-worms bobbing and dancing over the waves. As they got nearer they could see the glow-worms were the navigation lights of a tiny fleet of boats sent by the *Ocean* and other vessels now gathering at Corfu Harbour. They brought fire-fighting parties, powerful pumps, equipment for pouring foam to smother the oil fires, food, hot drinks—and renewed hope. Now the wounded were carried to the ship's side and lowered into the boats, each one with a label attached to him detailing his injuries.

It was a short but bumpy journey through choppy seas before they saw the flat-topped, slab-sided bulk of the *Ocean*. Its very size seemed comforting. The orders were for the carrier's doctors and sick bay attendants to give such treatment as they could until the hospital ship *Maine* arrived the following day. The carrier did not have special facilities for taking aboard large numbers of wounded but ingenuity and equipment designed for very different uses solved the problems.

As the little boats carrying the wounded came alongside, the carrier's huge crane lowered a metal tray down to a boat. These were the drip trays, measuring about eight feet by four feet, which were put underneath the aircraft to catch the drips of oil from the engines. Each wounded man lying on his stretcher was placed on a drip tray and hoisted up to the flight deck. There, parties of men from the carrier's crew waited to take them to the sick bay, or to the quarter deck, which had been turned into an emergency treatment centre.

As each man was hoisted up by the crane, a member of the boat's crew called out his injuries to the parties waiting on the flight deck, so that they would know how to handle him. Mr V. Lane, of Hoo, Kent, has a memory of this distressing part of the incident which has in no way been dimmed by the passing of the years. On that day in 1946 he was a naval airman, aged twenty, serving aboard the *Ocean*.

> I was on duty by the crane helping to get the stretchers on to the flight deck. Each stretcher was then placed on a trolley normally used for carrying bombs to be loaded on our aircraft. They were pushed to the forward aircraft lift on the flight deck and then lowered to the hangar below. Other parties of men then pushed the trolleys through the parked aircraft—Fireflies and Seafires—to the sick bay or the quarter deck. Each party had a sick berth attendant in it to ensure that the wounded were properly handled.

I still remember the feeling of distress—and anger—as I stood alongside the crane and heard the men in the boats shouting out the injuries of the wounded. 'This one has a broken back,' 'this one is badly burned,' and so on. We grew more and more depressed as the night wore on. We had been ashore with many of these men in various places and it sickened us to see them like this. The people responsible for laying the mines were roundly cursed in sailor fashion. Many of the wounded, like ourselves, had joined up as 'hostilities only' ratings. Many were in the groups for demobilization which had been 'frozen' for a time. I remember thinking that if they had been demobbed normally they would probably have been back home in the U.K. by then.

When all the stretcher cases had been ferried to the *Ocean*, the less seriously wounded followed. In their motley mixture of clothing, heads, arms or legs bandaged, they filed slowly up the gangway to the carrier's flight deck. For them, as for the stretcher cases, *Ocean* represented the safety they had at times thought they might never know. One man expressed that feeling as, on reaching the top of the gangway, he dropped to his knees and kissed the flight deck. Another survivor on the gangway behind him remembers: 'It was an involuntary, spontaneous gesture. I am sure we all felt like doing it.'

Another man had a double reason for thankfulness as he went aboard the *Ocean*. Serving aboard the *Volage* he had seen the *Saumarez* blown up and had blessed his own good fortune, for he had been transferred from the *Saumarez* a few weeks earlier. When *Volage*, too, was mined he quite naturally began to wonder what more Fate could have in store for him. Now, safely aboard the carrier, the relief at his own survival was tinged with the sadness of losing friends on both destroyers.

As the carrier's doctors, assisted by a Greek doctor and six assistants sent from a hospital in Corfu, began treating the wounded, the fire-fighting parties ferried out to the *Saumarez* were tackling the flames. The first party aboard the *Saumarez*

1. H.M.S. *Saumarez*, flotilla leader, early 1946.

2. H.M.S. *Volage* leaving Malta, 1946.

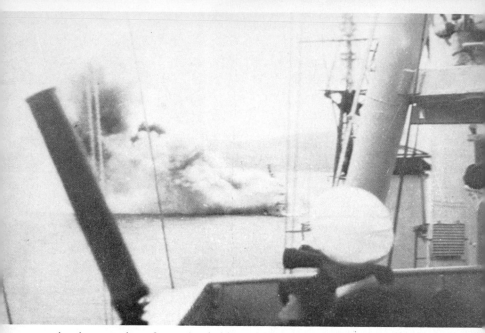

3. A picture taken from the bridge of H.M.S. *Mauritius* seconds after *Saumarez* struck the mine. Steam and smoke billow from her. Behind is the Albanian coast.

4. *Saumarez*, her steering gone, drifts helplessly, a plume of steam from the shattered boiler in her wake.

5. Blazing fuel oil brings a new peril to the *Saumarez*.

6. The *Saumarez*, blazing and down by the bows, drifts helplessly into a mine field off the Albanian coast.

7. Cordite blazes between A and B gun turrets of *Saumarez*.

8. A close-up of the cordite blaze as dusk falls.

9. The destroyers reach Corfu. From right to left—*Saumarez*, *Volage* (note the bows blasted off by the mine) and the cruiser *Leander*, which secured both ships to her stern.

10. A close-up of the shattered *Saumarez*.

11. This was the view which the *Saumarez* survivors had of the *Volage*, her bows blown off, as she towed her flotilla leader stern-first to Corfu.

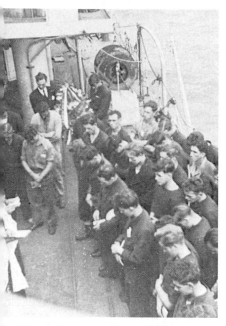

2. Some of the survivors of *Saumarez* at a memorial service for their shipmates aboard the destroyer.

13. Sick Berth Attendant P. A. Mitchell. He did heroic work among the *Saumarez* wounded.

4. A ship's boat takes urgent supplies to the *Saumarez*.

15. The funerals at Corfu cemetery. Teenage sailors carry the bodies of their shipmates.

16. This is the *Marjan*, the name-ship of a class of Yugoslav mine-layers, Also in the class were the *Meljine* and the *Mljet* which, the British Government alleged, laid the mines for the Albanians. When the Communists denied such ships existed, the British Government produced this picture from the authoritative *Jane's Fighting Ships*, but the Communists refused to believe a 'capitalist publication'.

was led by Lieut-Commander W. P. T. Croome, an air engineer officer aboard the *Ocean* and specially trained in fighting fires at sea. It is doubtful if any fireman, on sea or land, has ever set off to tackle a blaze in more incongruous gear—he was still wearing his mess kit. He recalls:

> As we neared Corfu I made my way to the flight deck to watch the fire party mustering to go on board *Saumarez*. Captain John was in debate with the engineer officer as to who should be in charge of the fire party. They apparently decided that all the marine engineering officers were needed on board the *Ocean*. They both turned on me and I found myself in the boat heading for the *Saumarez*, still in the mess kit I had worn at dinner.

One of the first things which Commander Croome saw as he clambered aboard the *Saumarez* was a remarkable example of discipline which impressed him deeply.

> The survivors were deeply shocked and I could get little professional help from them. They were, of course, completely exhausted, but I have a vivid recollection of the captain standing on his quarter deck, where he had obviously stood for hours with his messenger beside him, receiving reports on the situation and issuing orders. I was very impressed by the way in which every person, as he approached, gave a formal salute which was formally returned, before making his report. I still think of it as a remarkable display of discipline under stress.

Saumarez was still being towed slowly towards Corfu Harbour as Commander Croome took charge of the fire-fighting operations. He decided that *Raider* should cease her hosing-down operations. There was, he felt, imminent danger that *Saumarez* would be capsized by the weight of the water in her sagging forward section. He also had a personal reason for calling off *Raider's* attentions; he had just been drenched with water from her hoses and had been forced to take refuge in a sea-boat at the davits.

Commander Croome divided his men into two parties. One party was to tackle what remained of Number One boiler room, which was partially flooded with floating oil blazing on the surface, by filling it with foam. The second party was to try to fight their way forward of the damaged area. A fire in the signals office was tackled in an unusual manner—by pouring water down a voice-pipe so that it gushed out into the blazing compartment. But the fire had too great a hold to be controlled by this method alone. The fact that the men trying to subdue the fire in Number One boiler room were having some success showed in the fact that the deck above the boiler room no longer glowed red. But the party tackling the flames forward of the boiler room seemed to be making little progress. Commander Croome recalls:

> They were using spray nozzles on the hoses to disperse the smoke, but seemed reluctant to press forward into the messdecks. One difficulty I had was that, being sent aboard without proper warning, I did not have time to get to know the petty officers. Everyone was muffled up in damage control gear and wearing face masks and it was a problem to find out who was in charge of the groups of men.
>
> Another difficulty was that the parties were made up of naval airmen—aircraft handlers—who were young 'Hostilities Only' ratings sent out to relieve experienced men. They had a basic knowledge of aircraft fire fighting, but had never seen any real action before and were quite lost when it came to dealing with a fire below decks.

At one stage Commander Croome had to make a particularly difficult decision. The hoses which the crew of the *Saumarez* had been using and the extra hoses brought aboard by his own teams now became hopelessly tangled up on the upper deck and down below. It was like a 'ship full of snakes' and it was impossible to switch off any hose to transfer it to another part of the ship because of the difficulty of tracing which pump was supplying it. He decided that the only answer was to switch off all the hoses, sort them out and start again. He asked Captain Selby to give the order 'Still'. The hoses were then tidied up and the fire-fighting resumed.

'While we did so the fires rampaged again unchecked, but it was probably worth it.'

It was now almost two o'clock in the morning—the morning of 23 October. *Saumarez*, still being towed by the *Volage*, was in sight of the ships gathered in Corfu Harbour. *Leander* had completed her dash round the island and was preparing to secure the *Volage* and the *Saumarez* to her stern. *Mauritius*, with Rear-Admiral Kinahan, had followed the same route and was also in the harbour. Flood-lights on the upper decks of the cruisers and the *Ocean* lit up the sea in between them. Motor boats from the three ships chugged continually back and forwards taking further supplies, equipment and relief fire-fighting teams to the two destroyers. Despite the hour, crowds of people from the town of Corfu lined the ancient walls of the harbour to watch a day of disaster come to its close. As they peered into the darkness in the direction of the North Channel, they could just see two shadowy shapes, one glowing slightly, inching their way with painful slowness towards the illuminated *Mauritius*, *Leander* and *Ocean*. They seemed to be waiting, like three big brothers, to comfort two smaller ones. It was a sight which moved some of the women watchers to tears. And many of the men took off their hats.

Aboard *Saumarez* the fight to control the fire continued. Commander Croome and some of his men had managed to fight their way well forward. Commander Croome went farther forward alone, heaving a hose behind him, and found what he believed to be the seat of the fire at that time—a cordite fire in a magazine which supplied one of the forward 4.7-inch guns. He could see it glowing brightly down a hatchway in front of him. His initial inclination was to retire hastily. 'Then, from my early training, I recollected that cordite burns cheerfully in the presence of air, giving off acrid fumes. It does not explode unless confined and deliberately detonated. I was wearing a breathing mask, so I stayed where I was.'

Soon after 2.0 a.m. Commander Croome was relieved by another air engineer officer from the *Ocean*. His spirited leadership of the first outside help which *Saumarez* received had resulted in the fires being brought under control. He returned to the *Ocean* to rest and, no doubt, mournfully to inspect his one-time elegant mess kit.

Commander Croome does, however, admit to two errors he made while leading the fire-fighting team. Fortunately they were amusing rather than serious. The first incident makes it clear that *Ocean*, like *Saumarez*, had a sprinkling of public school boys among her lower deck ratings. After Croome had divided his team into two parties he had difficulty, as we have seen, in recognizing the leaders of each party because everyone was muffled up in protective clothing and breathing masks. He returned from an inspection farther forward and found 'each team being ably controlled by two well-spoken men who, I assumed, were sub-lieutenants and I treated them accordingly. It later turned out that they were National Servicemen who had the advantage of an education at Eton and the appropriate accent.'

At about this time a chief petty officer arrived by boat from the *Ocean* with food and a keg of rum to boost any flagging spirits. Soon afterwards Commander Croome noticed that the chief petty officer, who had joined the fire-fighting team, was staggering around. 'You're drunk,' the Commander said, and put him under arrest and sent him back to the *Ocean*. The C.P.O. protested his innocence and, fortunately, was able to prove that he was a life-long teetotaller. His unsteadiness and slurred speech had been caused by carbon monoxide poisoning from the fire fumes which had somehow leaked past his breathing apparatus.

More relief fire parties were arriving aboard *Saumarez*, and a member of one of them was air engineer Lane, who had been switched from his duties of getting the wounded aboard the *Ocean*. As he approached *Saumarez* he noticed a huge, jagged crack down the ship's side. The bows were swinging in a different motion from the rest of the ship—an unusual and not very pleasant sight for a sailor. This is his description of *Saumarez* as he saw her:

> When we went aboard we immediately made our way to where a lot of smoke was coming from. It was belching out from a hatchway leading to a messdeck up forward. The smoke was so dense we could not get down the hatchway, so a hose was directed into the mess through the hatch. Later one or two of us managed to get into the messdeck. The fire, we found, was mainly caused by burning clothing. One of us salvaged someone's best 'going ashore' uniform with its gold trimmings, and one chap in our party remarked that it would not be going ashore again. We took it in turn to play the hoses on the fire. One lad, on being relieved from his stint with the hose, was seen to raise his head from the black smoke, smoking a cigarette! This struck us as funny, but our laughter was not appreciated by an officer and we were told to get on with the job in no uncertain terms. Some of us went to explore the ship to see if anything else needed doing. Towards the stern of the ship were many bodies lying on the deck, dead or asleep—we did not stop to look. There were two reasons for this. If they were asleep we didn't want to disturb them. If otherwise, we didn't want to look.

It was now almost 3.0 a.m. One of the most remarkable voyages in the history of the Royal Navy was almost completed, and with the success which even those of the stoutest heart had, on occasions, doubted during the long night. *Volage* and *Saumarez* were now in the sanctuary of Corfu Harbour and aboard *Leander* the quarter deck party were ready to pass lines to the *Volage* and secure both battered ships to her stern. This was necessary because *Volage* could not drop her own anchors—for the simple reason that they had been blown to pieces by the mine.

Slowly *Volage*'s stern closed the stern of the *Leander*, held firm by her own anchor. Wires and a thick manilla rope were passed across the intervening stretch of water. One of *Leander*'s crew, getting a brief close-up look at the *Volage*'s tangled, truncated front as she wallowed in the choppy seas, remarked, 'God, it looks as though she's run into Beachy Head.'

The lines were secured and, as *Volage* drifted against the current and stretched them, a final check was made to make sure they were holding the two destroyers firmly.

Commander Paul glanced round his bridge party with a brief, tired smile. Like his, their faces were blackened with the smoke from *Saumarez* which the following wind had persistently blown across the bridge. The fumes from the blazing oil and cordite stung their eyes and rasped their throats. Their clothes, which had been drenched when the water-spout cascaded on the bridge, had now dried on their backs and reeked of oil and fumes. After a final glance at the *Saumarez*, wallowing and swinging drunkenly, but apparently securely, on her towing wires, Commander Paul leaned over the voice pipe to the engine room and said: 'Finished with main engines.'

The task was completed. In his first command, Reginald Paul had faced dangers and difficulties which some ship's commanders never see in a life-time at sea. They had been overcome by leadership and seamanship of the highest quality. Four times he had crossed into a minefield to try to save the *Saumarez*. He had surmounted the disaster to his own ship and, towing *Saumarez*, had successfully negotiated the mile-wide swept corridor and the narrowest parts of the channel. He had steamed stern-first for thirteen miles. Now, fourteen hours after leaving Corfu Harbour, the *Volage* and *Saumarez* were back, battered but safe, and Commander Paul could justifiably say: 'For what they are worth, I saved them.'

It was a feat of seamanship which, two years later, was to evoke a remarkable tribute from a most unexpected direction. On the afternoon of 29 November, 1948, Commander Paul was called to give evidence before the International Court of Justice hearing Britain's case, which blamed Albania for the mining of *Saumarez* and *Volage*, and the deaths and injuries to her crews. Like his flotilla leader, Captain Selby, he had, under examination by Sir Frank Soskice, Britain's Solicitor-General, and cross-examination by M Cot, the French lawyer conducting Albania's defence, to re-live the tragic events of 22 and 23 October, 1946. For both officers it was a painful experience. In a gesture whose gallantry contrasted sharply with the ferocity of his questioning, M Cot sympathized with both men in the deaths and injuries which their crews had suffered. But for Commander Paul there was a further tribute. At the end of the commander's formal evidence, Admiral Moullec, a French Naval officer acting as an expert adviser to the Albanian Government, rose to his feet to make his own sailor-to-sailor tribute. Facing the bench of eminent jurists from all over the world who were hearing the case, he said:

> You have before you, gentlemen, a great sailor. A sailor who conducted on that eventful afternoon very difficult manoeuvres with great courage, and I am sure that in a few years hence in all the naval schools' handbooks will be quoted a reference to the courage and initiative of Commander Paul on that afternoon of 22 October, 1946. His Majesty's Navy will be proud of Commander Paul.

Alas for fine sentiments nobly expressed. No one can doubt that His Majesty's Navy, and the country as a whole, had every right to be proud of Commander Paul, and of Captain Selby. Whatever pride the Royal Navy felt was expressed in the strangest of ways: when the honours list for The Corfu Incident was published it included the award of three medals for gallantry.* Neither Captain Selby nor Commander Paul received one. For them there was a King's Commendation.

It was as if the Admiralty, and the Government, wished to pull a quick and comfortable curtain over one of the most disastrous days in British naval history. And as for Commander Paul's courage and initiative 'being quoted in all the

---

* British Empire Medals went to Petty Officer Richards and Able Seaman Munton of *Saumarez* and Stoker Petty Officer Mitchell of *Volage*.

naval schools' handbooks' a few years hence, one can search a long time and never find the reference.*

The dawn of Wednesday, 23 October broke sombre and grey. To the crowds still lining the harbour walls of Corfu (and some had been there throughout the night) it seemed that this restrained colouring was in keeping with the picture displayed before them. Only seventeen hours before many had stood on the same walls waving their goodbyes as the four ships, paint gleaming and pennants and flags flying proudly, had steamed out of Corfu Harbour and headed for the North Channel. Now in the morning's first light they, and the crews of the ships which had hurried to give assistance, could see clearly for the first time what havoc those hours had wrought.

From the stern the *Volage* seemed completely undamaged. The *Saumarez*, her water-logged bows dipping into the restless seas, seemed intent on ending her agony by diving beneath the waves for ever. But aboard *Saumarez* there was little time for standing still to stare; there were still wounds to lick. Fire still burned inside her, although the powerful equipment and the expertise supplied by the *Ocean* was winning the battle which the destroyer's survivors had for so long fought alone. Some tried to snatch an hour or two of sleep, lying where they could on the upper deck, still in their sodden, oil-stained uniforms. Some could not change into clean uniforms if they had wished; all their spare gear had been destroyed in the forward mess-decks. Until they could be kitted out again they borrowed what they could from their mates.

There was no sleep for the Captain and his First Lieutenant; there were many matters still to be attended to. And the most distressing of these duties was the removal of the bodies which had been recovered. They were taken ashore by boats to lie, with the two bodies recovered from the *Volage*, in a tiny mortuary in Corfu. Later that day Petty Officer Hodges from *Saumarez* and Lieut Hicks Beach from *Volage* took a boat to

* The material available at the Historical Section of the Admiralty for the scrutiny of anyone interested in the incident can be contained in one foolscap folder with hardly a bulge. It consists almost entirely of an incomplete series of cuttings of newspaper reports.

the shore. Hicks Beach had a small flask of whisky in his pocket. I doubt if their respective captains would have objected if each man had taken a full bottle of spirits each, for theirs was a most harrowing duty; they had to identify their dead shipmates lying in the mortuary. In some cases it was not easy.

Back aboard *Saumarez* Lieut Gueritiz was 'doing his rounds' like all good First Lieutenants should. The fact that the ship was no more than a fire-blackened hulk did not alter routine. The fires were now out. The twisted and warped plates which had glowed red throughout the night were cooling. He had a word for each of the survivors as he passed along. Then he saw the Chief Bosun's Mate, his face grey and drawn, talking to the Torpedo Gunner, Mr Bannerman, who slapped the chief on the back and said, 'Come on, chief. Cheer up! Things aren't as bad as all that.' The chief turned on him, wincing with pain, and only the fact that the Torpedo Gunner was senior in rank saved him from a mouthful of ripe language and the chief from an act of insubordination. The chief had three broken ribs, caused when the explosion flung him against a bulkhead. He had told no one. He had worked throughout the night, driving himself to the point of exhaustion, although in considerable pain.

Captain Selby, too, walked round his once proud ship. For him, who had walked the bridges of destroyers all his life, it was like a self-inflicted torture. He made his way slowly towards the bows and stood immediately over the spot where the mine had exploded beneath his ship. The complete heart of the ship from the upper deck to the keel had vanished. Where Number One boiler room had been was now just empty space encompassed by jagged metal and twisted bulkheads. The whole forward section beyond the point of impact seemed to be hanging on by a thread. The only sound was an eerie creaking and groaning as the forward section rose and fell with the heaving sea—and the slosh of the water inside the ship.

And so the sad routines of the sorry day continued for *Saumarez* and *Volage*. Rear-Admiral Kinahan went aboard each ship, inspected the damage and talked to the survivors.

Clergymen from three denominations went out to the *Saumarez* and survivors still aboard the ship gathered together by the torpedo tubes, on the spot where they had laid their wounded. And there they held a short service of remembrance for their shipmates who had died, and prayed for the recovery of the wounded. They stood in a little group, heads bowed, weary from lack of sleep, their filthy oil-stained clothes contrasting sharply with the starched white robes of the clergymen. Wreaths of flowers were thrown into the sea, and into the blackened, water-logged cavern which had once been Number One boiler room. And as they mumbled the prayers, many a cheek felt the warmth of tears unknown since childhood.

Admiral Willis arrived from Piraeus and went aboard. It was becoming rather like a bereaved family receiving the condolences of friends—which, in a way, it was. The Admiral was accompanied by his flag lieutenant, a kind of personal assistant, who by tradition wears a rather ornate cord of gold over the shoulder of his uniform jacket. As he followed Admiral Willis aboard the *Saumarez* he took off the cord and put it in his pocket; this was, he felt, no time for showy trappings.

As Admiral Willis looked over the *Saumarez* and spoke to her crew, he kept saying, 'This must be heart-breaking for you.' He was deeply moved and to this day he remembers it as a 'terrible, deplorable business'. After brief discussions it was decided to tow the *Saumarez* and *Volage* to a quieter anchorage in the bay. Captain Selby left his ship to go to the flagship *Liverpool* to clean up. 'You look a bloody mess,' had been the robust reaction of the Commander-in-Chief's flag captain when he first saw Captain Selby. The 'bloody mess' was more considerable than he could have known. When Selby took off his clothes he saw for the first time that he was black and blue from his waist down with bruises he had received when he was blown around the bridge. But he remained on duty without a break for two days, refusing to 'stand down' until after the funeral when he went straight off to the hospital ship. It was then discovered that he also had three cracked vertebrae in his back. But, before he went off duty, he had one final distressing duty to perform—to prepare a report for the Board of Inquiry being assembled by Admiral Willis. Captain Selby's vast experience told him that his destroyer was so badly damaged she would never sail again; his report would, in a way, be her epitaph. Yet the language is restrained; no emotion appears among the words of a man who had just lost his ship and many of her crew. The report is printed as Appendix II on page 159.

When the hospital ship *Maine* arrived the wounded who required special attention were transferred to her. Other wounded men were taken ashore to a hospital in Corfu town. One of them was Lieut Knollys, navigator of the *Saumarez*, who had badly bruised kidneys and a gash over his eye. His injuries turned out not to be serious, but other sailors in the ward were fighting for their lives and, during the night, two of them died. The doctors and nurses were unstinting in the care and attention they gave to the British sailors. But for Hugh Knollys who, naturally, was not feeling at his best, even these warm-hearted ministrations became a little excessive.

'It seemed as though an endless succession of nurses arrived to take my temperature. I found this very boring and, after about the fourth one had rammed a thermometer down my throat, I fired off the only Greek phrase I knew. I can't remember what it was, or where I picked it up, but it had a miraculous effect and I wasn't troubled any further. When a doctor came to put some stitches in the cut over my eye I asked him about this. He spoke French, so we were able to converse. When I told him what I had said he fell about in the aisles with laughter and told me it was Greek for 'Beware, the cat is pregnant'.

In London, the Government, now aware of the full extent of the disaster, waited for some reaction from the Albanian Government. They waited in vain. From Tirana came not one word of explanation, let alone apology. But, more significantly, there was no repetition of the hysterical screams of outrage which had come from Hoxha when Britain had maintained the right of free passage through the Corfu Channel as an international highway of the sea. Now two warships had been blown up by mines inside what he insisted were Albania's own waters.

There were various courses open to Enver Hoxha. He could have called upon the Medzon Board to sweep the channel once again, recover any further mines and identify their country of origin. He could have protested to the United Nations and demanded that the country which had perpetrated this foul deed in Albania's own waters should be discovered and punished. But he did nothing and his silence was further circumstantial evidence of Albania's guilt, a silence forced upon him by the fact that he *knew* who had laid the mines in the swept channel. The Admiralty acted swiftly, for anyone prepared to lay mines in secret and then watch innocent ships run on to them would no doubt wish to remove the evidence of the crime. In Grand Harbour, Malta, Royal Navy minesweepers slipped their moorings and pointed their snub noses eastwards in the direction of Corfu, 500 miles away. The Admiralty meant to have that evidence for itself.

In Corfu that Wednesday evening, Greek workmen were digging graves in a corner of the cemetery of the English church: tomorrow the Navy would bury its dead.

Aboard the *Saumarez* on the Thursday morning, the handful of crewmen who had been left aboard still had duties enough to keep them busy. There was still wreckage to be cleared up. There were one or two compartments to inspect which had not been opened since the explosion. And, in addition, there was the problem of keeping away the boats which came from the shore carrying sightseers. They found this curiosity rather strange. 'Can't understand why they pay money to come out here to see us,' said one sailor. 'After all, you can't say we're a pretty sight.' But, among this little curious fleet were the hated 'bum-boats'. They are active in every major port in the world, ready to sneak alongside an unwary ship and filch what they can. Corfu was no different, although the men found it difficult to reconcile the activities of these bandits with the wave of kindness and concern which they had received from the rest of

Corfiot people. Those qualities were to be shown again that day at the funerals of the dead sailors.

Saumarez had her own private funeral that Thursday. And, in a way, the story behind it is one of the most touching incidents of the whole tragedy. When the mine exploded it jammed the door of the coxswain's office. The coxswain was among the survivors and, because no one else would be likely to be inside the office, it had not been opened. There were more important things to attend to.

Then one of the sailors left aboard got round to forcing open the door. Inside the wrecked office he found, lying on the deck, the ship's pet dog, killed in the blast. He had come aboard the ship in Malta as a puppy; his parentage was varied, but mostly terrier, and the crew adored him. He ate what they ate. And sometimes his uncertain steps around the upper deck suggested that someone had shared their rum ration with him.

The sight of the little dog lying dead was, for this young sailor, his own personal breaking point. For two days he had been surrounded by death and suffering. He had heard the screams of the wounded; his own chum was among those killed. Somehow the body of that defenceless little dog seemed to express the folly and frustration and futility of it all. An uncontrollable anger welled up inside him. He picked up the body of the little dog and hurled it over the ship's side into the sea. Lieut Gueritz had seen what happened. He went up to the sailor and said quietly, 'We can't do that. The dog deserves a decent burial.'

The dog had fallen between two catamarans—the big rafts which had been secured alongside *Saumarez* to make it easier for boats to tie up. A leading seaman took out one of the *Saumarez* boats, scooped up the dog and took him round to the other side of the ship, facing the open sea. And there they gave him 'a decent burial'.

That afternoon ten of the men who died were laid to rest. They were accorded the only tribute the Service could now give them—a full Naval funeral.

But, just before it began, there occurred an incident quite

out of keeping with the solemnity and sadness of the occasion. The hundreds of men from the ships of the fleet who were to attend the funerals were ordered to muster at an assembly point in Corfu town. Then they would be detailed off to march behind the cortege. Captain Selby ordered Lieut Wells-Cole to go to the assembly point and supervise the attendance of the mourners who were closest to the tragedy—the survivors of the *Saumarez* and *Volage*. Some of them who had lost all their gear had not yet been re-kitted; they were still wearing odd pieces of clothing lent to them by shipmates. Captain Selby, with that refreshing directness of manner which was so much part of his character, told Wells-Cole, 'I don't care if some of our chaps *do* look like pirates, they're still going to attend the funeral.'

When Wells-Cole arrived at the assembly point he saw that the Fleet Gunnery Officer was supervising the assembling of the men. As soon as the latter saw the *Saumarez* and *Volage* parties he roared out, 'Fall out those men.' The Fleet Gunnery Officer was senior in rank to Wells-Cole. But, mindful of his strict instructions from Captain Selby, Wells-Cole took the highly unusual step of reversing a senior officer's orders. 'Fall *in* those men,' he ordered. And the survivors in 'unofficial' uniform shuffled back into their places. Then followed a heated discussion between the two officers, in which each pointed out that he had received his orders. Eventually the men were allowed to stay in the ranks of the mourners, a decision which saved further embarrassment all round.

Admiral Willis, who had arrived with Captain Selby, witnessed the latter stages of the incident and, after the funerals, asked Captain Selby if Wells-Cole had undergone a hospital check-up since the mining of the *Saumarez*. When Captain Selby said that, to the best of his knowledge, he had not, the Admiral suggested he should do so. Wells-Cole was sent to the *Maine*. It was discovered that when he was blown against the director tower his skull had been fractured in three places. For two days he had been in a semi-conscious state, unknown to himself or to anyone else. And that finally explained why he had ignored Stopford's plea for help with the trapped petty officer, and his highly unusual actions at the funeral.

And so the sad proceedings could begin, with the mourners from the *Saumarez* and *Volage* taking their rightful places. A firing party of ten sailors, one for each of the victims to be buried that day, led the procession through the narrow streets of Corfu town. Behind them came the Royal Marine band, their muffled drums tapping out the mournful beat of the slow march. And behind them came hundreds of sailors from the ships of the fleet, headed by Admiral Willis.

The people of Corfu shared their grief. The route was lined with men, their heads bared, and women wearing black lace shawls over their heads. Little boys walked alongside the firing party, trying to keep step with the slow march. Through the streets of the old town they marched, streets only just wide enough to encompass the marchers and the accompanying children. The route took the procession along the sea-front road overlooking the harbour. And beyond the harbour, like a sinister backdrop, was the coast of Albania. The ten coffins, each borne by eight bare-headed sailors were carried into the churchyard. As the mourners gathered round the graves, the sun broke through the clouds, casting long shadows from the cypress and ilex trees. A brief service conducted by padres of three denominations, the volleys from the firing party, and it was over. The men drifted slowly back to the boats waiting to take them to their ships.

The following day there was another service for two men who had died of their wounds. They were buried alongside their shipmates and over each grave was placed a simple white cross, bearing the date of death, the name and rank, and the name of the ship. They lie together by an old stone wall. Down the years the graves have been beautifully kept. Every year gladioli splash their vivid colours among the crosses, relieving the sombre tints of the ilex and cypress trees, and occasionally sprays of flowers, simple and anonymous, appear in this 'corner of a foreign field that is forever England'.

A fortnight after the funerals the Admiralty had to take one name from the list of wounded in the incident and add it to those who had died. It was the name of Petty Officer Zarb, one of the Maltese cooks who served the officers' wardroom. He should not have been aboard *Saumarez* when the destroyer sailed from Malta with the rest of the Fleet, but the man who was to take over his duties had not arrived and he had to do 'one more trip'. He was badly burned in the explosion, but not as severely as some of his shipmates. Yet he seemed to make little progress towards recovery. He was transferred to Bighi Hospital in Malta, not far from his own home, and there other survivors in the hospital worried about his lack of progress. It seemed as if he had just accepted that what has to be has to be. He died on 4 November. His death was the last revision to the casualty list—forty-four killed.

The funerals of the twelve men marked the beginning of the end of the tragedy as it was played out in Greek waters. But, before the last ship sailed from Corfu harbour, many matters of considerable moment were dealt with and, when the minesweeping flotilla arrived from Malta, there were to be further moments of high drama.

One of the pressing decisions which had to be taken immediately after the disaster was the future, or the fate, of the two destroyers. The fleet depot ship *Ranpura* had now joined the other ships in the harbour. Inside her capacious bulk was the machinery and equipment needed to patch up the two destroyers so that they could be towed back to Malta for repair— if repair were practical or possible. The ships were moved from their quiet anchorage, the tow lines which had saved the *Saumarez* from further disaster were slipped and the destroyers were secured one on each side of the *Ranpura*. They looked a pitiful sight, lying against the protective sides of the former liner. One man who was there said, 'It reminded you of a mother with her arms around a couple of children who had been in a scrap.'

After Navy construction engineers had inspected the damage, senior officers, headed by Admiral Willis, met to discuss the next course. The *Volage* presented no problem. With the bulkhead immediately aft of her damage firmly shored, she could be towed stern-first to Malta. *Saumarez* was a much more difficult problem. Her bow section, hanging on to the rest of the ship 'by a thread', made her unstable even in calm seas. If gales, or even heavy seas, blew up on the voyage to Malta she would almost certainly capsize. It was decided that the bow section should be blown off with explosives and the rump of the destroyer then towed to Malta. This decision was a bitter disappointment to Captain Selby. It is a matter of pride with every ship's commander that, if his ship is damaged, he somehow gets her into port. If *Saumarez* were to return to Malta, her home port, he wanted her to enter Grand Harbour just as she was, showing all her wounds, not as a truncated travesty of a flotilla leader. He felt that *Ranpura* had the machinery and the expertise to make this feasible. He suggested that *Ranpura* should pass stout wires under the bow section, haul the two parts of the ship together again with winches and then secure the wires. With the bows firmly 'tied on' in this way, she too could be towed back to Malta. Captain Selby himself could not undertake the voyage because of his back injury, but First Lieut Gueritz certainly was prepared to do it and he had gone so far as to 'thumb a lift' for *Saumarez* from a frigate which was returning to Malta and was prepared to act as a tug. The idea was turned down; the forward section was far too fragile, said the construction engineers. Later events were to leave the engineers wondering whether their dogmatic attitude had not made them look rather foolish.

It was during these discussions that an incident occurred which, by its bad taste and bad timing, caused acute embarrassment and anger. No final decision had yet been made about the *Saumarez* and, during a pause in the talks someone volunteered what he felt was a humorous remark. 'There is one thing we could do,' he said. 'We could take part of the *Saumarez*, part of the *Volage*, stick them together as one ship and call it H.M.S. *Sausage*.'

None of the people who was there can now remember—or does not wish to say—who made that unfortunate remark. It can be safely assumed that none of the officers involved in the events which had cost forty-four lives would have been guilty. But, who ever it was, became well aware of his unfeeling indiscretion by the anger which showed clearly on Admiral Willis's face, and by the embarrassed foot shuffling silence which followed it.

But there were moments when laughter in the right place, even by the wounded aboard the hospital ship, could be enjoyed. And the ubiquitous Corfu turkeys once again figured in a hilarious happening. Most of the *Saumarez* ship's company had been moved to other ships, leaving only a skeleton crew and an officer, who took turns to be on duty.

The main task was to deter by any legitimate means (and mildly illegitimate if not observed by authority) the bum-boats which were forever hovering around. Some of the occupants of these boats had managed to get aboard the *Saumarez* and had stolen various items of equipment. They had even swiped personal possessions of men who had been taken off the ship.

One evening the walking wounded aboard the *Maine* were enjoying a film show on the hospital ship's upper deck. During the show Lieut Edge-Partington of *Saumarez*, and others sitting near the gangway, saw a naval rating staggering up the gangway carrying two or three large sacks. He was followed by Lieut O'Riordan, the doctor of the *Saumarez*. Edge-Partington remembers:

'The rating dumped the sacks on the deck. The officer of the watch said: 'What are these?' and he was about to give the sacks a kick when they moved. Then they moved again—a sort of jerky movement. The doc had reached the upper deck by now and the officer of the watch again asked what on earth was in the sacks. 'Torty torkeys,' said the Doc triumphantly. The officer of the watch could not understand his Irish accent and the Doc had to explain carefully that the sacks contained thirty turkeys.*

* This incident is well remembered by many of the survivors. However, suggestions as to the number of turkeys which Dr O'Riordan brought aboard range from twenty to eighty! The author has settled for the figure recalled by the doctor himself.

They did indeed, and Dr O'Riordan insisted that they were taken to the galleys and served up as a special treat for the wounded. But hearing of *the way* the Doc got those turkeys gave the wounded as much pleasure as the eating of them. Aboard the *Saumarez* earlier that evening, watching the bumboats waiting to pounce if the watch slackened, he realized that there was a grave danger that the Corfiots in the boats would eventually get what they wanted. Royal Navy canvas, the best in the world, is greatly sought after in every port from Hong Kong to Gibraltar. So the good doctor did a deal. He sold the destroyer's quarter deck awning—canvas, wire supports, securing ropes and all—for the thirty turkeys. He said later, 'If the awning was going to vanish I didn't see why the lads on the hospital ship shouldn't have something out of it.'

It was, of course, a highly illegal act and the doctor would have had no defence if authority had decided to investigate the mysterious disappearance of the awning. But a 'Nelson's eye' was turned on the incident and the wounded were left to enjoy their turkey dinners. It was refreshingly irreverent incidents like this which had earned Dr O'Riordan the nickname of 'The Mad Irishman'.

On 28 October *Volage* set off on her stern-first voyage back to Malta, with a minesweeper, the *Clinton*, and a fleet tug, the *St Day* to share the towing duties. Captain A. W. Clarke, C.B.E., D.S.O. and Bar, had been ordered by Admiral Willis to undertake the responsibility of getting the destroyer back to Malta, for her regular skipper, Commander Paul, was ill with sand fly fever. It was to prove an adventurous passage. The little convoy of three ships sailed from Corfu, this time heading southwards. Once clear of the protection of the land, a rising wind and a nasty sea made the *Volage* heave and buck. The shored-up bulkheads behind her shattered bows groaned ominously and Captain Clarke decided to return to Corfu and wait for better weather.

The following day they set off again and found that smoother waters made towing much easier. The *Clinton*, however, did have difficulty in making headway with her ungainly tow, and she had to have some assistance from the engines of the *Volage* going astern. Any increase in wind velocity made the towing operation particularly difficult as *Volage* swung wildly at the end of her tow rope. It was during one of these periods of difficulty that *Volage* found herself inside, of all things, a minefield, one of the many in the area still waiting to be swept. But she emerged unscathed.

To try to control the wild swinging it was suggested to Captain Clarke that the crew should fix up a steadying sail at the stern of the ship—in reality the bows. On the basis that it could do no harm and might even help, he agreed and the crew rigged up canvas awnings as sails. The enterprise did, in fact, prove of considerable help and, in this unsightly and undignified way, *Volage* proceeded in more sedate fashion and finally reached harbour on 1 November.

Back in Corfu work went ahead on the 'amputation' of the bow section of the *Saumarez*. The fleet salvage officers decided to perform the operation by putting what is called a necklace of explosives round the bows and then exploding it. A series of small charges explode simultaneously and usually give a nice clean 'cut'. *Saumarez* was towed out of Corfu harbour, well away from any shipping, and the necklace was placed over the bows and fixed around the 'good metal' astern of the damage area.

Watchers from the attendant ship saw a spout of white water engulf the bows and heard the roar as the charge went off. When the spray subsided they saw—the bows of the *Saumarez* still attached to the rest of the ship. Clearly the destroyer, which the construction engineers said could not possibly undertake the journey to Malta, was made of sterner stuff than they imagined.

On close inspection they found to their amazement that the explosives which they were quite sure were sufficient to detach the bows from the rest of the ship, had merely perforated her with a series of small holes. 'Rather like a piece of toilet paper', said one of the officers.

The whole operation had to be repeated. This time it was

successful, and the bows which the destroyer had so bravely pointed at the *Scharnhorst* sank beneath the sea for ever more. To rid the *Saumarez* of the damaged forward section, quite literally hanging on by a thread, had taken as much explosive as was contained in the mine which damaged her—a remarkable tribute to her builders, Hawthorn Leslie of Wallsend-upon-Tyne.

Saumarez, like *Volage*, was eventually towed back to Malta stern-first. Unlike *Volage*, she was never to sail again under her own steam, for it was judged to be uneconomic to repair her. But strangely enough, she did live on—and in a way which made that unfortunate remark about H.M.S. *Sausage* partially come true. For weeks *Saumarez* lay in Malta Harbour while, in the dockyards, workmen were building new bows on to *Volage*—an intricate task completed with great skill. And some of the fittings from *Saumarez* which had escaped damage were built into *Volage*. *Saumarez* was eventually towed back to Britain where, like many a proud ship before her, she was broken up for scrap.*

Gradually the armada of ships which had assembled in Corfu began to disperse. Some of them went on to Argostoli to take part in the belated fleet regatta. Other units of the Mediterranean Fleet were preparing to sail once again into the waters of the North Corfu Channel to carry out a minesweeping operation. As these preparations went ahead, Enver Hoxha broke his silence. On 30 October, eight days after the mining of the destroyers, it was revealed that he had sent a telegram to the Secretary-General of the United Nations, Mr Trygvie Lie, protesting in the strongest terms against what he called 'the unauthorized penetration of British warships into Albanian waters'. The information came, as one might expect, by courtesy of a friendly propaganda organization—the Yugoslav News Agency.

The telegram declared that four British warships entered Albanian waters at 1.0 p.m. on 22 October with the intention of

* Detailed histories of the four warships involved in The Corfu Incident are given as Appendix III.

'attempting to provoke incidents'. It was, the message continued, a violation of Albanian sovereignty and it was also the second case within a short space of time of British warships entering Albanian waters without authorization. The last remark was a reference to the incident involving the *Orion* and *Superb* the previous May.

This fine display of injured innocence then continued:

> On the same day (22 October) and the following day several three-engined British planes flew over Albanian territory between the villages of Muzine and Radat without authorization of the Albanian Government and with the aim of intimidation and provocation.
>
> On the same day two British planes circled three times at low altitude over the port of Saranda.
>
> The Albanian Government strongly protests before the General Assembly of the United Nations against these repeated provocative interventions, directed against our people, who have fought and made such sacrifices for the common cause of the Allies. The Albanian Government demands an intervention from the Secretary-General to put an end to such provocations.

The reader will notice one glaring omission from this burst of indignation—any reference to the severe damage to two British destroyers on the date in question—damage undoubtedly caused by explosions inside Albanian territorial waters—or to the deaths of forty-four British sailors. The Communist Government of Enver Hoxha may well have been new to the arts and artifices of international diplomacy, but clearly it was learning fast. For to have admitted any damage to the British destroyers would have required some explanation for the explosions. And that they had no wish to give. The alleged violation of their air space was more worthy of protest, and more convenient. In the face of this piece of specious pleading the British Government maintained the aplomb of a nation with centuries of diplomatic breeding behind it.

'The Foreign Office,' reported *The Times*, 'takes the view

that Albania has no grounds for her protest. The Corfu Channel . . . is an international Channel, and has been for a great number of years.'

The Times, well-briefed by the Foreign Office, was, of course, correct in its interpretation of the view of the British Government. But dispassionate observers will be left to wonder at the difference between 'intimidation and provocation' (the Albanian view of the events of 22 October) and Fleet movements organized with the express intention of seeing 'whether the Albanians have learned to behave themselves'.

The British Government refused to be intimidated by this belated and blatantly ludicrous protest. Preparations for sweeping the channel went ahead and Albania was told just that. Diplomatic niceties such as penetrating, for the third time in six months, what Albania claimed as her own territorial waters were considered only to the extent of what offensive action Albania might take. The evidence of Albania's murderous deceit was there, eleven feet beneath the waters of the Corfu Channel. The Government intended to secure that evidence and the Admiralty was ordered to guard its minesweeping fleet with such forces as it thought necessary. The result was that, on the morning of 12 November, the Royal Navy assembled an impressive array of naval power off the Albanian coast.

En route to Albania the gun crews and fire control parties had carried out exercises. For, once again the Navy was prepared to fire back if fired upon, and once again Admiral Kinahan was in charge.

Details of the operation—code-named Operation Retail— had been worked out in close consultation between the Admiralty and the Foreign Office. Its aims were twofold: to make the Medri Route safe for shipping and, if possible, to recover one or more of the mines for identification. In an attempt to save herself from any allegations of malpractice the British Government insisted on the whole operation being witnessed by a neutral observer, so Commander Mestre, the French delegate on the Medzon Board, was hurriedly flown out to join the fleet.

On that dull, grey day, as the escort ships steamed in a protective formation a few miles off the coast, the minesweeping flotilla of Commander Q. P. Whitford chugged towards the area to be swept. On the bridge of his own ship, *Welfare,* Commander Whitford studied the Albanian shore for any signs of activity. There was none. No sign of Albanian troops, no sign of the gun emplacements observed by *Saumarez* and *Volage,* not even a peasant gazing out to sea at this massive array of foreign force. It was as if Albania, fearful of what might be found, had decided not to look.

Commander Whitford led his little force of sweepers, *Skipjack, Seabear, Truelove* and *Sylvia,* and some smaller sweepers for dealing with the shallow waters, into the narrows of the channel. Small buoys were laid to mark the area to be searched —a twelve-mile oblong area opposite the port of Saranda. By the time the search area had been defined and marked darkness came and the sweepers and their covering force retired to open waters for the night. On the following day they returned; again it was a grey day with occasional rain squalls; again the Albanian coast was quiet and still, as though the whole territory had been evacuated. With the sweeps out, the force, led by *Welfare,* chugged along the first of the twelve-mile laps from Cape Kefalu in the North, past Saranda to the end of the sweep at the entrance to the narrows in the south. On the bridges of the ships, all eyes were on the seas above the underwater sweeping gear, waiting for the sight of a mine bobbing to the surface. Suddenly a huge roar echoed around the mountains and a plume of water reared up and over the *Seabear*. A mine had exploded in her sweep. Observers aboard the sweepers now saw that what had seemed to be an abandoned land certainly was not so. For the roar of the explosion brought scores of heads popping up from the hitherto apparently unmanned defences. Albanian forces had been watching all the time. The explosion was immediately opposite Saranda Bay and, almost at once, a second mine was caught in the underwater sweeps and came bobbing to the surface. Commander Whitford ordered small boats to secure the mine and, under the neutral eyes of Commander Mestre, it was towed to a bay on the Corfu coast and de-fused.

On the second lap of the sweeping operation eight more mines were cut, and on the third lap a further twelve, but Commander Whitford made it clear in his official report that he could not categorically state that there were no more in the immediate area. But twenty-two mines were enough for the British Government; they proved their case that the mines had been recently and deliberately laid. The evidence was overwhelming. All the twenty-two mines were inside the supposedly clear Medri Route. They covered the positions in which the *Saumarez* and the *Volage* were damaged. They were a deliberate 'lay' by a ship or ships steaming on a clearly defined and accurate course. The 'lay' was three miles long running from north-west to south-east across Saranda Bay, and curving southwards at the bend in the channel; who but the Albanians would lay mines outside their own port?

That they had been in the water only a few weeks was proved when the first two mines to be recovered were examined by Lieut Phillips, the mine disposal officer for Operation Retail. He rendered them safe and personally dismantled them. The black paint with which the mines were coated was in mint condition. There was fresh red paint on the horns of the mines. The mooring wires were still coated with layers of protective grease. When Commander Mestre unscrewed the horns of one of the mines they came away easily. There was no evidence of stiffness of the threads, or rusting, which would have been present if the mines had been in the water for a long time. Finally, there was not one barnacle or one strand of seaweed on either of the mines.

Commander Whitford and Lieut Phillips, both vastly experienced in dealing with mines, concluded that they could not have been in the water for more than two months. That meant they must have been laid on or after 13 September.

Feelings ran high aboard the minesweepers as the crews saw mine after mine bob to the surface in a channel which had been declared safe. The tension was reflected in the eagerness with which they fired rifles at the mines to try to sink them. At least they were firing at *something* which bore the hand of the 'enemy'. But their efforts were restricted by orders that on no account was firing to be directed towards the Albanian coast. Despite all that had gone before, the British Government was abiding rigidly by its decision to avoid unnecessary provocation. This order, and the difficulties of manoeuvring in narrow waters meant that only three of the twenty-two swept mines were exploded in this way; the remainder drifted on to the Albanian shore and, presumably, were quickly spirited away by the Albanian authorities. Certainly they were never seen again by Western eyes.

The anger which the minesweepers' crews felt is referred to in Commander Whitford's official report of the sweeping operation. At the end of this report, a detailed account of the events of 12/13 November, he added what he described as 'a postscript'. The views he expressed had certainly not been canvassed by the Admiralty. Indeed it could well be observed that he was exceeding the duties required of him in appending them. The fact that he did give his views is clear evidence of his strength of feeling on an emotional subject.

> All personnel have been warned that they are to make no reference to the operations, beyond the fact that they have been on a normal mine-sweeping operation and that mines have been cut. Although I am confident that this order will be loyally obeyed, I now wish to draw attention to the fact that the circumstances attending the mine-cuts are well known to officers and ratings of the mine-sweeping force, including the fact that the mines were cut in an international channel and that they had obviously been laid recently. There is a strong feeling of anger and resentment against whoever may have been responsible for this callous disregard for human life, which has resulted in the death of so many British seamen. Many officers and men have expressed the opinion, which I share, that an early official statement of the facts is

most desirable, even if it is not possible definitely to attribute the responsibility to any particular nation or persons.

In fact Commander Whitford's request for a speedy statement was unnecessary. On the evening of 13 November, only hours after the completion of Operation Retail, the Admiralty announced that twenty-two moored mines had been found in the Corfu Channel and two of the mines had been taken away for expert examination. It added that a full report was awaited from the Commander-in-Chief, Mediterranean.

That report, when it was received at the Admiralty in London, fully confirmed that the villain of the Corfu Channel incident was without doubt the Albanian Government of Colonel-General Enver Hoxha. The task now was to prove it to the world; to show Enver Hoxha and his men to be what the evidence, in the British Government's mind, clearly showed them to be—no more than a bunch of murderers.

It was to be a battle of millions of words, many of them bitter and most of them, from either side, displaying an intransigence born out of each side's passionate belief in its own case. The Albanian case was also to be marked by perfidy, prevarication—and an infuriating facility for refusing to recognize any fact which remotely reflected against them. This latter facet, as practised by the skilled diplomats of Russia, was even then showing itself and dimming hopes that the partnership of East and West during the war could be carried on into peace.

The battle of words was to range across the world—from New York, to The Hague, even inside the secret frontiers of Albania itself. Britain's objective was threefold; reparations for the damage to the two destroyers; compensation to be paid to the relatives of the forty-four men killed, and to the wounded; and a clear statement of Albania's guilt. This second stage of the battle was to last for three years. The victory, when it finally came, was pyrrhic indeed.

What was the reaction back home in Britain to The Corfu

Incident? The answer to that question is a sad, even a shaming one, which even today rankles in the minds of the survivors. To the everlasting shame of Britain the death or mutilation of nearly 100 young men raised barely an eyebrow, certainly not the howl of outrage which it deserved. The newspapers gave the incident scant coverage and soon forgot it in the midst of the numerous post-war controversies. In Parliament barely a voice of protest was heard.

The reasons for this cold, apparently cynical, disregard are not easy to interpret logically, for one of our national characteristics is to honour, even to revere, sacrifices made by fighting men in the service of the country. The vital clue is in the date of the incident—22 October, 1946. For six years Britain and her Allies had fought and finally won a war which had taken the greatest toll of any struggle in history.* But now peace was here and Britain claimed it as a right earned by suffering and blood.

The cynics explained the sudden, hectic rush to the conference chambers around the world on that new persuader, the atomic bomb. Certainly the new shape in our lives, the Mushroom Cloud, and the knowledge of the new dimension of horror which it had wrought at Hiroshima and Nagasaki, fed this frenetic desire to forget the past and get on with the peace. It could be seen in the blind faith being placed in a new organization—the United Nations. The fact that its predecessor, the League of Nations, was itself born of similar hopes and yet collapsed, was dismissed as an historical irrelevancy. It failed, people said, because America lost faith with it. This could not happen with the United Nations because America had turned her back on comfortable isolationism, and had given solid

---

* The total casualties in the First World War amounted to some 10,000,000. The Imperial War Museum in London puts the casualties in the Second World War at between 15,000,000 and 50,000,000. The reason for this wide-ranging estimate is the greater involvement in the Second World War of civilian populations. It has, for instance, been extremely difficult to estimate accurately the number of civilians killed during the war in Russia, or the number of Jews massacred by the Germans. But the total figure is certainly nearer the larger estimate than the smaller one.

proof of this by having the United Nations building permanently in New York.

In Britain people showed their hunger for peace in a personal and cruel way by spurning the one man who, above all, had given them the chance to enjoy it—Winston Churchill. The Labour Party, surprising even itself, won the first post-war General Election and Winston Churchill found himself sitting on the Opposition benches in the House of Commons. The overwhelming national desire to forget the war cannot be better expressed than in that one fact. It is in the light of this conscious amnesia that we must judge the reactions, or rather the lack of them, to the events of 22 October.

The day after the disaster, when its magnitude became clear, Mr J. Dugdale, Parliamentary Secretary at the Admiralty, rose to make a grim statement to the House of Commons. It was couched in words such as many a war-time disaster at sea had been broken to the Commons and to the nation. To the M.P.s sitting in the Chamber it must have sounded uncomfortably reminiscent.

The Times on 24 October published a report of the brief exchange in Parliament. It also carried on its news pages a report of the incident. It comprised a brief statement from the Admiralty about the casualties and some details from *The Times* correspondent in Athens, which added little of significance to Mr Dugdale's statement in the House of Commons.

Now *The Times* had always been accepted, both in this country and abroad, as a most accurate 'barometer' by which to judge the mood and feelings of the British people on any current situation of importance. Indeed, in 1946 some foreign Governments believed that *The Times* spoke officially for the British Government of the day. We can, therefore, by studying how *The Times* and its readers reacted to a peacetime disaster with such sinister undertones, deduce with some accuracy the feelings of the country about it.

The report measured eight inches in length. The headline was across just one column of the page. The report was, in fact, only one and a half inches longer than the coverage given in the same issue to a birthday concert by the Fleet Street Choir.

The leader columns of *The Times* are also an accepted guide to the major issues of the moment on domestic and international affairs and, therefore, worthy of editorial comment. On this occasion the paper which, in its heyday, earned the nick-name of 'The Thunderer' for its courageous, outspoken comments, could not even raise a whisper over the deaths of forty-four British sailors. Not a word about the disaster appeared in the leader columns.

But if one takes the view, as many do (but not the author) that it is a newspaper's duty to reflect public feeling, not to influence it, *The Times* was correct to treat the incident with scant feeling and even less concern. The evidence for this view is to be found in the Letters to the Editor columns of *The Times*, another reliable guide to public feeling. Not one letter on the subject was published; the British public as a whole confessed itself utterly unmoved.

Other newspapers reported the incident to a greater or lesser degree, but public reaction was similar to that shown by readers of *The Times*. There was no anger, not even interest. The author recalls clearly how this apparently callous lack of concern by people at home angered the crews of the four ships involved. That it still rankles is shown by the remarks of survivors of the *Saumarez* and *Volage* who have written to me. It was also shown at a unique reunion, twenty-five years after the incident, of officers who served aboard the *Saumarez* at Corfu. The author was privileged to attend this very personal occasion, which was arranged by Rear-Admiral Gueritz. Among those at the reunion was Rear-Admiral Selby. As the reminiscences flowed these officers found the massive national apathy to the deaths of their shipmates still a topic for discussion, though in sorrow rather than anger.

How could a nation which, down the centuries, has so stoutly supported its fighting men that even defeats have become invested with the pride of victory, so cruelly turn its back? In the years since 1946 the British public has been ever ready, and rightly so, to pay full tribute as British forces faced the post-war phenomenon of the rising tide of nationalism in Malaya, Kenya, Cyprus, Aden, Ulster. Yet, even in 1949, when Albania stood convicted of what was tantamount to a charge of murdering forty-four British sailors, the reaction in Britain was the same cool disinterest.

It is a fact that the British public, if it seemed to care little about the incident, was helped in this attitude by the minute amount of information it was given. Whether it was a deliberate policy of the Admiralty and the Government to hush-up the events of October, 1946 may never be known. But it was the result, if not the conscious intention. Certainly it was hardly in the interests of the British Government in general, and the Admiralty in particular, to over-publicize an incident which had ended so disastrously.

Geography also played its part in dampening down public reaction to the incident. Albania was, and still is, one of the 'unknown' countries of Europe. Corfu was just another Greek island.

But the third reason for the public attitude was certainly the most powerful. It was simply that Britain was sated with war. For the first time the bomber had brought the full horror of modern conflict quite literally into the homes of millions. For the first time the British people knew devastation of their homes on a scale which the French had suffered twice in thirty years. The determination that it must never happen again had the powerful reinforcement of personal involvement. And look! cried this national voice of hope, pointing to New York. On 23 October, 1946, the very day the British public was getting the first sketchy details of the Corfu disaster, the new hope of world peace was opening its General Assembly in New York—the United Nations.

There, standing before the delegates of the world to welcome the United Nations to its permanent home, Harry Truman, President of the United States, had summed up the feelings of millions with the words: 'The people of every nation are sick of war. They know its agony and its futility. No responsible Government can ignore this universal feeling.'

Again *The Times* no doubt judged the mood of the nation correctly when it allocated space in the newspaper to the events of the day. In the main position of the paper forty-seven inches of space were devoted to the opening of the General Assembly and President Truman's speech. The report giving the first news of serious casualties to British sailors in the Corfu Channel was on the same page. It will be recalled how much space it was given—eight inches.

To a nation which could put names to some of the most horrifying moments of all history—London and Coventry; Hamburg and Dresden; Buchenwald and Dachau; Hiroshima and Nagasaki—words like *Saumarez* and *Volage*, Corfu and Albania were an unwanted intrusion into the plethora of peace which overwhelmed the country.

Yet on that day in 1946, many things happened which a nation could have acclaimed with pride, if it had so desired.

There were numerous acts of courage. There were feats of superb seamanship. And, in the end, there were the dead and wounded who sacrificed and suffered for a cause about which they had been told little and understood less.

Did ever men give so much for so little recognition?

3

The End of the Affair

B RITAIN'S first shots in the battle of words which
followed the incidents of 22 October came early in
December. Inevitably they came in a manner which had,
down the centuries, presaged the most cataclysmic moments
of history—the diplomatic Note of Protest. Because Britain
had no ambassador in Tirana—it will be remembered that this
question was under review immediately before the Corfu
incident—the Note was handed to the Albanian minister in
Belgrade, the capital of Albania's ally and confidante,
Yugoslavia.

It protested about the incidents of both 15 May and 22
October and referred to the mining of the *Saumarez* and
Volage as 'displaying the most callous indifference to the safety
of international shipping'. The Note marshalled the evidence
in the possession of the Government, which pointed the finger
at Albania as the guilty party. It stated its case for an apology,
reparation and compensation. Then it departed from all the
accepted canons of diplomacy by putting a limit on the time
the Government was prepared to wait for a reply—fourteen
days. And if a satisfactory answer was not received by then
'His Majesty's Government will have no alternative but to bring
the matter before the Security Council of the United Nations
as a serious threat to, and a breach of, international peace and
security, showing criminal disregard of the safety of innocent

seamen of any nationality lawfully using an international highway.'

If the British Government inserted the time limit in the protest Note because it felt the Albanian Government might buy time by procrastination, subsequent events were to prove that this was a tactic the Albanians would frequently adopt. For that reason it was justified. But it is interesting to note that it is a ploy rarely used among mature nations; there are rules even about falling out.

The reply, in fact, was delivered two days late—on Christmas Day, 1946. It contained a complete rejection of the claims made by the British Government. It dismissed any allegations about mines damaging British destroyers as unconfirmed and rejected any suggestion that Albania could be held liable for any damage to the destroyers. Britain's claim that the mines were so close to the Albanian shore that she must have laid them herself—or possess the knowledge of who laid them— was dismissed with contempt. It must have been the Greeks, was the suggestion; they are always stirring up trouble.

Having given an ultimatum and a time limit the British Government had left itself no room for manoeuvre, if indeed any kind of manoeuvre or new initiative would have achieved the results desired by Mr Attlee and his ministers. The threat to take the matter to the newly formed 'safety valve' on international disputes, the Security Council of the United Nations, would have to be implemented. Early in the New Year the Cabinet met to review the situation and the Foreign Secretary, Mr Ernest Bevin, reported on the latest developments. A decision to go before the Security Council was taken and, on 10 January, 1947, Britain's formal complaint was lodged with the Council. It took Albania another eleven days to reply to the discussions in New York—she was not represented in the United Nations—but this was only the start of another round of prevarication. Time after time discussion of Britain's charges had to be put off because Albania's observer, Mr Kapo, her Minister in Belgrade, had not arrived in New York. What Albania hoped to achieve by these obvious time-wasting tactics, apart from time to prepare her case, is difficult to understand. In any event, it was not until 19 February that Mr Kapo was finally installed in the conference chamber and Britain's delegate, Sir Alexander Cadogan, could present the Government's case against Albania. Quietly, with hardly a flourish and certainly with no histrionics, Sir Alexander ploughed through the brief so carefully prepared and documented by the Foreign Office and the British staff at the United Nations. He reviewed the whole affair, from the badly aimed shells in May to the carefully placed mines of the following October and the damage and casualties which had occurred. He stressed Britain's fervent desire to settle a most blatant aggression in a peaceful way, and he cited in this respect Britain's restraint under the greatest provocation—two cruisers fired upon, two destroyers mined with resulting heavy casualties, yet not one shot fired by any British ship.

If Sir Alexander, by his restrained tone and delivery, hoped to set his opponents an example of calm appraisal of the facts, he was soon to be disappointed. Mr Kapo rose to present the reply of his country and to make it immediately clear that Europe's weakest nation would be in no way over-awed by Europe's strongest. Not for him the calm, clinical analysis of the trained diplomat. From the first word to the last his speech was a hotch potch of rambling vituperation. All the injustices against his country down the years—arguable or blatantly invented—were paraded before the Council as though *these* were the matters which delegates should be discussing and the question of the *Saumarez* and *Volage* and forty-four dead British sailors were matters which did not concern Albania. Britain, not Albania, was the aggressor. His Government had declared the channel closed to all shipping, unless Albania had given permission for the passage. If ships came to harm while sailing through these waters, well, that was their fault. They had been warned. The minesweeping operations carried out by the Royal Navy on 12 and 13 November were further examples of Britain's aggresive intentions against his country. Delegates who wondered how making waters safe for the shipping of all nations could be interpreted as an act of aggression were soon to learn that, according to the standards of Albanian logic and debate, this was eminently possible. Mr Kapo sat down, no doubt feeling confident that, back home in Tirana, Comrade Enver Hoxha would be pleased with his delegate's first assault on the debating chamber far away in the West. He had admitted nothing, he had apologized for nothing, he had retracted nothing. And, in the view of many of the delegates, if constructive thought be the art of negotiation, he had said nothing.

But, even so, Mr Kapo's words were as milk and honey compared with the tirade launched by the delegate from Soviet Russia, Mr Gromyko. This young career diplomat gave the delegates of the West an early indication of the intransigent and devious opponent he was to be for decades to come. The first few minutes of his speech dispelled any doubt Mr Kapo might have felt about Russia's intention to support Albania all the way. As the quality and intensity of that support was revealed, it left Mr Kapo positively beaming. Mr Gromyko rejected Britain's allegations against Albania with a scorn which seasoned diplomats were not used to hearing. He saw a plot of the most sinister kind in the fact that Albania was not represented on the Medzon board of the Mine Clearance committee, due entirely, he said, to the intransigence of the Western nations.

Saumarez and *Volage*? Forty-four British sailors killed? What warships? What casualties? Mr Gromyko refused, on the word of the British delegates alone, even to believe that an incident had taken place. And then, like a lawyer pleading in a libel case, he added quickly that if there had been an incident such as was claimed by the other side, Albania was not to blame. His whole attitude was that he would not even believe the nose on Sir Alexander's face were his own, on the mere claim of Sir Alexander. The Security Council had yet to celebrate (or ponder ruefully over) its first birthday and, already the pattern of polarization between East and West was set. Gone, so quickly and for ever it seemed, was that cosy euphoria of the immediate post-war era with its promise of peaceful co-operation. The hand-shaking between Russian and Allied soldiers across the smouldering rubble of Berlin had now become fist-waving.

To try to break the deadlock between the two sides in the dispute the Council decided to set up a three-nation committee of 'neutral' nations to hear further evidence from both sides. The committee's claim to complete neutrality can, however, be judged by the fact that Mr Gromyko insisted upon, and finally won, the right to have Poland, a member of the Communist bloc on the 'neutral' committee. The two other members of the committee were Colombia and Australia.

For day after day the two sides argued their case before the committee. And as the words flowed the accusations of Mr Kapo became more and more wild and the quality of his argument more and more juvenile. He finally descended to the kindergarten level of logic in one particular passage which had committee members looking at each other in incredulous disbelief. Mr Kapo had already said, for the umpteenth time, that Albania had not laid any mines, and that, *if* the two ships *had* been mined the damage had probably been caused by mines from nearby fields laid during wartime and inefficiently swept (by Britain, of course). Then he put forward his second theory —*that the mines could have been laid by the minesweepers of Operation Retail.* No wonder the British delegates were dumbfounded. Mr Kapo was actually suggesting that the mines which killed forty-four British sailors on 22 October were, in fact, laid three weeks later by other British sailors! If at this moment, when such specious nonsense was offered before such an august body, Sir Alexander gave up all hope of gaining anything by intelligent argument, he might be forgiven. But he carried on manfully, answering the wildest statements by Mr Gromyko and Mr Kapo quietly and calmly. Finally, after four weeks of such frustrating activity, the neutral committee reported back to the Security Council. The four weeks of argument had been wasted. The committee had failed to reach agreement. There was, in fact, unanimity on one point—that two British warships had been damaged with the loss of forty-four lives. The Polish representative predictably did what Mr Gromyko expected of him by saying there was no evidence to support Britain's accusations against Albania. Dedicated students of the Communist *modus operandi* would judge Albania's foray into international affairs an unqualified success. Propaganda, the seeking of it and the dissemination of it, are powerful weapons in the armoury of the men of Marx and Lenin, to be used at all times to the confusion of capitalism. Mr Kapo had seized his opportunity well. For a month he had occupied the stage in New York, the heart of capitalism, thrusting his vituperations down the throats of the delegates, forcing his nation's case into the bourgeois Press and the radio networks, parading with a mixture and venom and glee all the well-worn anti-capitalist slogans—and inventing a few new ones for good measure. Even Stalin himself had reason to be proud of this representative of his latest satrap.

Faced with the inability of its committee to find a way through the impasse of widely divergent views, the Security Council met again and, on 25 March, 1947, voted on the issue. For the British delegates, harassed and harangued for a month, it seemed a clear-cut and tangible victory. By seven votes to two the Council found Albania guilty of knowing about the mines in the Corfu Channel and, therefore, responsible for the deaths of forty-four British seamen. The seven votes in support of the British case came from the United States, Australia, Belgium, Brazil, China, Colombia and France. Mr Gromyko and Dr Lange, the Polish delegate, voted against the resolution, and Syria abstained.

But, even then, total victory was snatched from the hands of the British delegates. Mr Gromyko could not now win this stage of the battle but he could frustrate the victors. He did so by using what was to become the dirtiest four-letter word in the world of international diplomacy—the veto. When the constitution of the United Nations was drawn up the veto— the right of any of the five permanent members of the Security

Council to nullify a majority decision—was built in to protect the five Big Powers from annoying or embarrassing proposals by small powers. Russia turned it into a double-edged sword by 'ratting' on the four other Big Powers and using the veto to her own personal advantage. As the differences between East and West became more and more intense down the post-war years, the veto became Russia's inevitable weapon of frustration.

But, back in 1947, the Western Powers were only just beginning to realize what a potential for mischief they had given to a nation which obviously was not prepared to play the game as it had been intended. Russia had not used the veto since the previous September, when the United States proposed an on-the-spot investigation of the Balkan situation. Now Mr Gromyko again threw his diplomatic bomb into the chamber, Dr Aranha of Brazil, the Council President, announced that, as the resolution had failed to obtain the concurring vote of a permanent member of the Council (Russia) it was lost. Even though Britain had been denied a clear-cut victory, she had won a moral battle of significance. By a clear majority the Security Council had supported her resolution which declared that 'laying mines in peacetime without notification is an offence again humanity' and that the mines in the Corfu Channel 'could not have been laid without the knowledge of Albania'.

The ultimate aims of Britain's diplomatic battle—a clear statement of Albania's guilt, an apology and compensation—remained unsatisfied. Despairing of direct negotiations with Albania, the British Government decided to take the case before the International Court of Justice at The Hague. When Sir Alexander recommended this course of action to the Security Council it brought a final flurry of injured innocence and indignation from Mr Kapo and Mr Gromyko. The Council, by eight votes to two, dismissed their protests and agreed with Britain's request.

And so on 9 April, 1947, the Corfu Incident was sent for

adjudication before the highest court of national morality this side of the Judgment Seat. The story entered its final phase.

* * *

From the moment on 13 November, 1946, when the mines were found in the Medri route inside Albanian waters, the British Government, through the Admiralty and the Foreign Office, proceeded to assemble its evidence of Albania's guilt with all the skills and many of the techniques of a Scotland Yard team of detectives investigating a particularly vicious murder. And that was exactly the way The Corfu Incident was viewed, even though, for reasons of diplomatic etiquette, the Foreign Secretary, Mr Ernest Bevin, at times seemed to play down the affair with words which for some seemed far too honeyed for the situation.

The circumstantial evidence pointing to Albania's criminal involvement was already damning in the eyes of reasonable men. But events of the last few months had shown that Albania and her supporters were far from reasonable. Men who would not accept that two destroyers had been blown up and forty-four men killed because they could not see the jagged metal, or touch the white crosses in the graveyard, would be equally vicious in the battle of words.

Piece by piece the evidence was built up. Firstly a piece of metal found on the *Volage* was sent to metallurgists and they reported that it appeared to be a piece of the casing of a mine and, in fact, was identical in type to the metal of the mines swept up in the Corfu Channel.

Marine biologists studied the cable and casing of the two mines recovered for traces of marine growth. They studied the movements of the tides in various parts of the Mediterranean. They studied the rate at which marine growth fouls under-water objects—it varies greatly in different parts of the Mediterranean—and came to the conclusion that the mines had been recently laid.

But where had the mines come from? They were identified as being German mines of the GY type which had been laid by the thousand in the Mediterranean. They were monsters—the biggest mines used by any side during the war—containing six hundred pounds of explosive and weighing more than a ton. The reader may wish to pause here and reflect that it took the same amount of explosive to detach the bows of *Saumarez* from the remainder of the destroyer. A clue to the immediate ownership of the mines was found on the casing—a swastika painted in white. It was known that the Germans, as they retreated from Yugoslavia, had left dumps of these mines behind and it had been the custom of the Yugoslav authorities to mark these captured mines with a white swastika to denote their German origin.

But were any of these captured mines in existence in the area at the time of the incident? Here the investigators so painstakingly building up Britain's case were able to call on documents captured from the Germans. At the end of the war, in accordance with the surrender terms, all German documents were handed over to the Allies. Among this vast array of records, covering Germany's war effort on every front, was a set of papers handed over, on 11 May, 1945, by Captain Albertz, Chief of Staff to Admiral Loewisch, Germany's Naval Commander (South) in the Mediterranean, to Commander E. R. D. Sworder, a member of the Central Mine Clearance Board. The papers were the stock lists of German mines in the Mediterranean. Port by port they recorded the number of mines, and the various types, in stock at any given time. As the Germans retreated these stocks were abandoned and taken over by the liberated countries.

The stock lists showed that, on 25 April, 1945, there were no less than 1,800 mines held in store at the port of Trieste. More significantly, 171 of these mines were of the GY type. And it was in April that the Yugoslav troops of Tito, defying an agreement made with General Alexander, the Allied commander in Italy only two months previously, occupied the port of Trieste. The mines, therefore, clearly fell into the hands of the Yugoslavs. The stock books also showed that about 300 mines were held at Fiume in February, 1945. At the time it was the duty of the various military commanders in these captured areas to arrange for the disposal of seized war material.

But the British investigators, searching for the minutest scraps of evidence to build up their case, were unable to find any record in the German documents that any GY mines had come into the possession of Albania in this way. They did, however, discover that none of the mines came into Britain's possession. The stock lists also showed another significant fact —that no GY mines were listed as being held in ports in Greece. The Foreign Office believed—rightly as events were soon to prove—that the Albanians and the Yugoslav's would try to switch the blame for the Corfu Channel Incident on to Greece. Albania and Greece had for years been feuding over disputed lands in the border area and Greece was an obvious target. The fact that she possessed none of the mines in question was a useful piece of evidence to be used to destroy that argument.

The big question—and the one which defied all efforts to provide an answer was: *Who had laid the mines?*

Albania could not have done so herself; she did not possess the ships. Despite Albania's wild accusations, there was nothing to suggest that they had been laid by Greece. In any case, all Greek naval units were under the overall control of the British Commander-in-Chief at the time. As the process of elimination continued it became increasingly clear that only Yugoslavia had the mines and the ships equipped to lay them. But did she have a motive? Here again the answer was damning. She had a *double* motive—her close associations with Albania and her new-found hatred of Britain regarding the Attlee Government's attitude over Trieste.

This Adriatic port had been a predominantly Italian city for years. Its seizure by Tito's partisan guerrillas was a distinct embarrassment to Britain, who intended that it should be handed back to Italy after the war. Pressure from the two Western Powers forced Tito, despite the support of Russia, to quit Trieste, and the city and the area around it was declared a Free Territory. It was divided into zones—Zone A, including the port and the town, was administered by the British and the Americans. Zone B, to the south, was controlled by the Yugoslavs. This arrangement was viewed by Tito as nothing more than a carve-up between Britain and America. Trieste would maintain its essentially Italian association and eventually, he feared, revert to Italy. This favouring of a defeated enemy and the ignoring of the claims to the city of a nation which had fought to defeat both Germany *and* Italy, drove Tito to a state of anger just this side of the epileptic. In speech after speech he denounced Britain. His Partisans, still mobilized and now seeing a new enemy, roamed the hills in the Yugoslav-controlled Zone. And occasionally trouble erupted in the city of Trieste itself. The situation was at this time so tense that Britain and America took it in turns to have a powerful warship in Trieste harbour, her main armament facing the city at all times. One of the first duties of *Leander*, on leaving the waters of the Greek islands, was to undertake this watchdog surveillance in Trieste. So Tito's Yugoslavia was certainly no lover of Britain or of things British at the time of The Corfu Incident.

The second side of Yugoslavia's double motive was equally compelling. When Albania achieved her long-fought-for independence the association between Yugoslavia and Hoxha's kingdom was no more than one of emotion. Tito was pleased to have a Communist ally, even a new and a very weak one, on his doorstep. Hoxha was equally pleased to bask in the admiration and affection of his boyhood hero. Over the ensuing months this platonic association evolved until, at the time of the incident, Albania and Yugoslavia were as close together as lovers have a right to be. Tito, acting on the instructions of Stalin, who was also delighted to see a new Communist enclave establishing itself in the capitalist West, showered money, materials and advice on the ever-grateful Hoxha.

Albania's Budget for 1947 was bolstered with a credit from Yugoslavia of the equivalent of £10 million—no less than 56 per cent of the total Albanian budget for the year. Military assistance was equally generous. Arms and military supplies flowed into Albania, and with them went Yugoslav instructors to train the Albanian army. Selected members of the Albanian forces were sent to Yugoslavia for training.

In the diplomatic field, Yugoslavia looked after Albania's interests in every country where Hoxha's Government was not recognized.

This increasingly voluptuous embrace was finally consummated on 9 July, 1946—a little more than three months before The Corfu Incident. At a ceremony in Tirana the two countries signed a Treaty of Mutual Friendship and Assistance. Its every paragraph declared the closest political and military co-operation. Article Three of the Treaty, for instance, pledged each country to come to the assistance of the other in the event of a threat to independence or territorial integrity. It received, not surprisingly, a unanimous vote of ratification in the People's Parliament of Albania and, in a fulsome speech, Hoxha described the Treaty as 'a powerful basis for the eventual defence of the independence and integrity of both countries'. And he added: 'At this solemn moment we feel happier and stronger than ever because we have done our duty in the great cause of humanity and because, in Yugoslavia, we have a strong ally who will back our cause as we back theirs.'

The degree of economic co-operation between the two countries can be clearly seen from the text of an Economic Agreement signed on 27 November, 1946. The opening sentence declared unequivocably: 'The contracting parties agree to co-ordinate the economic plan of their two countries *on a joint basis.*' Clearly, in the autumn of 1946, relations between Albania and Yugoslavia were as close and as friendly as it was possible for contacts to be between two independent powers.

Was it not reasonable to suppose that, when Albania resolved to close the Corfu Channel to all 'unauthorized' shipping, she would decide that the only effective way of doing so would be to lay mines, and the only country to whom she could turn to for help was the country with the mines and the minelayers— Yugoslavia?

That was the reasoning of the British Government as,

towards the end of 1947, it began to document its case for presentation to the International Court. It lacked, however, one vital fact, without which it could never be regarded as completely damning; one positive, incontrovertible piece of evidence that Yugoslavia had laid the mines. Britain's case, expressed in a voluminous mass of detailed statements by witnesses (including the captains of *Saumarez* and *Volage*), the evidence of numerous experts, Admiralty charts, photographs and affidavits, was overwhelming. But it was entirely circumstantial. There was no evidence of Yugoslav minesweepers being anywhere near the Corfu Channel at the material time. The army of men around the world who had worked so hard, and sought so diligently, to build up Britain's case consoled themselves with the thought that very rarely do the police catch a murderer actually with the weapon in his hand; many a killer had been hanged on circumstantial evidence less compelling than the case Britain now put before the International Court.

The laborious procedure of the Court, in which both sides to the dispute studied each other's written evidence and made a reply to it, was now set in motion. Copies of the mountains of documents and statements were made for the perusal of the fifteen judges from all over the world who comprised the court.

It was not until 26 February, 1948, that the legal representatives of Britain and Albania finally faced each other in a court of law and it was to be almost another nine months before one word of Britain's evidence was heard. Once again, Albania and her legal representatives indulged themselves in delaying tactics of the most obvious kind.

One such tactic, which resulted in many weary days of argument and counter-argument will suffice to show how juvenile was the Albanian attitude. Her legal representatives, without any prior warning, suddenly submitted that Britain had no right to bring the case before the court. The reasoning behind this puzzling proposition was that the rules of the United Nations said *both* parties to a dispute should agree to take their quarrel before the court. And, while the United

Kingdom had agreed to do so, Albania was not a willing participant. All this despite the fact that Albania herself, in a letter to the court, had previously said that she fully accepted the recommendation of the Security Council that the dispute should be referred to the court. Oral arguments on this preposterous smoke-screen took six days of public sittings followed by a long, time-wasting recess while the judges deliberated upon their verdict and had it printed, in English and in French, for all to see. There was even a minority judgment from Judge Daxner of Communist Czechoslovakia, which, of course, came down on Albania's side.

But the main verdict went against Albania; it had taken weeks, and a forty-eight page statement of the judgments, to settle a matter which any judge of the British High Court would have dealt with in a couple of hours. In fairness to the judges of the International Court, lest it be thought that they stand accused of dilatoriness and inability to recognize a sharp practice, let it be said immediately that The Corfu Channel Incident was the first major case on which the court had deliberated. Throughout the world great hopes were placed in it as a 'safety valve' tribunal where nations, to use Churchill's phrase, could 'jaw jaw and not war war'. The permanent judges were anxious that, through the Corfu Channel case, they would establish a reputation of fairness and impartiality that would sustain the court for years to come. Fair and impartial—and patient beyond measure—they certainly were throughout, as the case dragged on from months into years. The fact that the court has, to all serious purpose, ceased to function effectively, cannot be blamed on the judges who administered its first big test.

And then, as these tedious arguments echoed round the court room at The Hague, there occurred an incident so dramatic that, if a novelist or film writer had presented it to his public, any credibility he at that moment possessed would have vanished in a flash. It was revealed that a 'mystery witness' had been discovered who would give sensational evidence for Britain. The timing of this revelation added to the sudden air of melodrama. On 9 November—the day the case against Albania was really to begin with a powerful opening statement by Sir Hartley Shawcross, the morning newspapers had all the drama they needed. 'Mystery witnesses' and 'eleventh hour' revelations are the stuff of which newsapers are made. For the first time in two years The Corfu Channel Incident rated more than a paragraph or two.

The *Daily Herald*, for instance, talked of a 'closely guarded mystery witness' waiting to give evidence which had come to light since the case began. So important was his evidence judged to be that, the paper added, the man 'has been kept under guard since he arrived at The Hague, and has not been allowed in town without an escort'.

The story of this mystery witness goes back to 16 July, 1947. On that day an open boat sailed into the harbour of Bari, in Southern Italy. There was just one man in the boat and he said he had sailed across the Adriatic from the port of Sibenik in Yugoslavia. The voyage, he said, had taken him almost three days. In Bari he contacted the British consul and the story he told this startled official was so amazing, and obviously so important, that he sent the man to Rome to repeat his narrative to the British Ambassador there. The Ambassador, well aware of The Corfu Incident and of the attempts to seek justice at the Security Council and the International Court, also realized that here was evidence which, if it were true, could be legal dynamite. The man from Sibenik was passed on to London to repeat his story once again—this time to Foreign Office officials and officers of Naval Intelligence.

He was, he said, Karel Kovacic, a Lieutenant-Commander in the Yugoslav Navy since before the war. Recently he had incurred the displeasure of the Communists who were now in control of his country and he had felt that sooner or later his life would be in danger. These fears were amply confirmed, he said, when quite by chance, he happened to see his '*characteristica*'—a confidential report on his attitudes and behaviour—which had been compiled by a fellow naval officer who was the political commissar at the Yugoslav naval base at Sibenik.

It was this officer's task to keep a close watch on all the officers, particularly those who had served (as Kovacic had served) in the old *Royal* Yugoslav Navy and, therefore, might be out of sympathy with the new régime. This *'characteristica'*, which the officer had most unwisely left lying in his desk, stated that he judged Kovacic to be 'reactionary-minded' and not prepared to 'transfer his technical knowledge to other people'. In Yugoslavia at that time the charge of being reactionary-minded meant imprisonment or death and Kovacic was prepared to risk neither for a régime which he hated.

So, at the first opportunity, he sailed from Sibenik to Bari to tell his story. At Sibenik Kovacic had been in charge of the signal workshop and stores. Before that he had served at sea during the war. On 16 or 17 October, 1946—he could not be entirely sure of the date—two small vessels of the Yugoslav Navy sailed into Sibenik. To Kovacic they were old friends, the vessels *Mljet* and *Meljine*, for he had served on both of them as navigating officer when they were engaged in laying mines. They were also adaptable as minesweepers and it was in this latter duty that they had recently been engaged. Kovacic was instructed to carry out repair work to the signal systems on both ships and this work began on the day after they arrived. Almost immediately, on 17 or 18 October, Kovacic received contrary instructions by telephone. As a matter of urgency he must carry out temporary repairs to the signal equipment and get the ships out of his hands as soon as possible. This sudden change of orders puzzled Kovacic, for the amount of work which was really required was quite considerable. But he changed his instructions to his workmen and, by three o'clock that afternoon, the temporary repairs had been completed and the ships immediately sailed for another part of the base. About an hour later Kovacic left his office and went by motor launch to Sibenik town. As the launch passed Panikovac Cove, a small inlet, he saw the *Mljet* and the *Meljine* lying alongside the jetty. They had their sterns towards him and he could see that both ships had been fitted with mine-rails, the 'railway lines' on which mines trundle over the sterns of minelayers and drop into the sea.

About thirty mines had already been loaded on to each ship. They came from a tunnel where Kovacic said he knew mines were stored. Men were still busy loading more mines on to the vessels and, as Kovacic's launch chugged on past the cove, he actually saw a mine winched on to one of the vessels. All the mines were large, contact mines. Kovacic recognized them as mines of the German GY type. They had their contact horns, containing the firing mechanism, fitted. And he could see that they were marked with a swastika.

The effect of this information on Kovacic's listeners in London can well be imagined. Later that evening, Kovacic saw the *Mljet* and *Meljine* again in Panikovac Cove. By this time they appeared to have been loaded with their full complement of mines—about forty to each vessel.

The following morning, when Kovacic returned by launch from Sibenik town to his office at the naval base, he saw that the *Mljet* and the *Meljine* had gone. During the night they had sailed away. The date was almost certainly 17 October—five days before the incident. The departure of the minesweepers-turned-minelayers puzzled Kovacic. From his own experience he knew that at the time every available minesweeper throughout the Adriatic was engaged on sweeping the thousands of war-time mines which still infested shipping routes and entrances to ports. Why should two ships which had been engaged solely on this work suddenly be converted to laying mines, loaded up and sent off into the night?

Kovacic busied himself about his duties at the naval base and thought little more about the departure of the two ships—until he heard a BBC radio broadcast in his own language which told of the disaster which had struck the two British destroyers three hundred miles to the south. His suspicions became, in his own mind, near certainty four days after the destroyers hit the mines. On his regular early morning journey from Sibenik town to his office—he always tried to be there by 7.0 a.m.—the launch once again chugged past Panikovac Cove.

Kovacic saw that *Mljet* and *Meljine* were back. As they had slipped away on their mission so they had returned, under the cover of darkness. And now there were no mines to be seen on the upper decks.

A few quick sums told Kovacic that by leaving on 17 October the two ships would have had ample time to steam to the Corfu Channel, lay the mines and be away from the area before the Royal Navy sailed from Corfu town. Allowing for navigating through the islands off the Dalmatian coast, and around the minefields still in existence, Kovacic estimated the distance from Sibenik to the North Corfu Channel and the Albanian port of Saranda as 350 miles. The *Mljet* and the *Meljine* could steam at six knots, giving them ample time for the voyage, even if they had to stop to refuel.

And Kovacic had even more evidence to offer. The departure of the *Mljet* and the *Meljine* so soon before The Corfu Incident, and their return so quickly afterwards, left profound suspicions in his mind. Cautiously, being well aware of the presence of political commissars searching out any sign of Western affiliations, he began asking a few casual questions around the naval base. One man to whom he spoke was a sub-lieutenant engineer aboard one of the minelayers. This man volunteered the information that, after leaving Sibenik on the night of 17 October, the two ships headed south. They refuelled at a Yugoslav port in the Gulf of Kotor and then continued south to undertake what the officer described as an important duty. At that point the officer, no doubt also becoming aware that he was saying too much, refused to reveal anything further about the ship's mission.

Kovacic, risking his very life to find confirmation of his suspicions, spoke to another officer who had sailed on this secretive mission. And he said that the 'important duty' to which the sub-lieutenant engineer had referred was the laying of mines in Albanian territorial waters. Kovacic lived with this information for ten months. He told no one of his suspicions. Indeed, whom dare he tell? Then, in 1947, when he learned he had been marked down as a 'reactionary' he decided to escape while he had the chance, seized the small boat and sailed the 200 miles across the Adriatic to Bari to tell his story to the British authorities.

In London he was questioned in the closest detail about his story. He was asked to account for times, dates and names of people mentioned. He seemed to hold nothing back. Nor, equally important, did he appear anxious to gild his evidence to make it appear the more plausible. His motives, too, seemed sound enough. He knew he would not be able to return to Yugoslavia again and had no real desire to do so. He had nothing to gain and nothing to lose.

By this time Britain had already submitted in detail the Government's statement of claim against Albania. Kovacic's evidence could not, therefore, be included as part of that case. In fact the British Government kept Kovacic's story a complete secret for more than a year. During that time Albania's definitive Reply to Britain's case against her was received. It amounted, as was expected, to a verbose and vituperative denial of any involvement in the disaster.

Throughout the spring and summer of 1948, the perpetual procrastinations continued at the International Court; minor points of procedure were invested by the Albanians with a status which far transcended any importance they might have possessed.

Then in the autumn of 1948, only a few weeks before the real face-to-face confrontation on the facts was due to take place in the court-room, Britain dropped a bombshell. The legal adviser delivered to the International Court, as they were obliged to do, the Government's Rejoinder to Albania's Reply. It contained, in addition to the arid counter-arguments, a devastating new element—the complete story as told by Lieutenant-Commander Kovacic, late of the Yugoslavia Navy.

Why did the British Government wait until this late stage in the proceedings before revealing this new evidence? Officially, the reason was twofold.

First, the Government was not obliged, under the rules of the International Court, to reveal this new evidence until it submitted its Rejoinder to Albania's case. Secondly, it would have been wrong to submit the evidence until it had been checked and verified, so far as was possible.

Both statements are entirely true. But court-room confrontations are frequently planned with all the detail and precision of a set-piece battle. And, in both war and law, the element of surprise is frequently a most valuable weapon. The effect of Kovacic's story on Albania's case was to prove devastating, even though there was no immediate evidence of this. No word of reply came from Tirana or Belgrade but one can easily imagine the activity, the telephone calls and the frantic cables humming across and between the two countries, as attempts were made to check the truth of Kovacic's story.

The facts were easy to discover. Formulating strategy to discount them evidently took a little longer. The Yugoslavs and the Albanians delayed until only a few hours before the major confrontation at The Hague in putting out a statement, via the Government-controlled Yugoslav radio. Before Commander Kovacic had the chance to utter a word before the International Court, Tito's radio was denouncing him as a liar. His story of seeing two ships setting off from Sibenik loaded with mines was just not true; therefore his story about their returning empty was equally false.

The statement, which was later submitted as evidence before the International Court, described Kovacic as a 'Yugoslav army deserter'. It further said that he escaped from Yugoslavia 'with the aid of a Foreign Intelligence Service'. And, in an attempt to nullify Britain's surprise tactics of keeping Kovacic's evidence a secret until the last possible moment, it said Kovacic had defected eighteen months previously and gave evidence in Britain after appearing 'on 4 October last'. In fact, as we have seen, the British case was that he first told his story to the British consul in Bari soon after he landed in Italy, repeated it to the British Ambassador in Rome and then, in London soon afterwards, repeated and enlarged on his narrative. The reference to 4 October was presumably meant to be the date on which Kovacic made out the affidavit putting his story into writing. This affidavit was then handed to the Court and, according to the rules, shown to the Albanians.

On that morning, as those people in Britain who could muster any interest in The Corfu Incident were reading about the 'mystery' witness, the judges, counsel, advisers, witnesses and all the host of people making up the secretariat of the International Court were assembling for the opening session in the Great Hall of the Peace Palace in The Hague.

Britain paraded a most distinguished array of legal eminence before the judges on the bench. In addition to Sir Hartley Shawcross, who was to present Britain's case, there were Sir Eric Beckett, legal adviser at the Foreign Office (he would deal with matters of pure law), two professors of law, one from Oxford University and one from Cambridge, and two promising young barristers, Mr R. O. Wilberforce* and Mr J. Mervyn Jones.

'May it please the Court . . .' With those five words, the traditional start to the presentation of a case in the courts of Britain, Sir Hartley began his opening statement. They presaged millions more in the months to come. Sir Hartley's initial statement alone contained more than 50,000 words. He was on his feet for two days, marshalling his facts and presenting them to the court with all the clinical skill and eloquence which, until he became Attorney-General in the Attlee Government, had earned him one of the highest incomes known at the Bar at that time.

As he described the ill-fated voyages of the *Saumarez* and *Volage* the judges studied charts of the North Corfu Channel and track charts showing the courses the ships steered through the swept corridor. Photographs taken from the *Mauritius* seconds after the *Saumarez* struck her mine brought the agony of that moment two years ago right on to the judges' bench. On a chart displayed in the court-room the judges could see the positions of the mines recovered from the Channel by Operation Retail.

Britain's case, that the two ships had struck mines recently

* Now Lord Wilberforce, a High Court Judge.

laid in the channel with the full knowledge of Albania, was 'really overwhelming'. Sir Hartley's final words of his opening speech to the court were:

> I can imagine nothing which would make a greater contribution to the rule of law in international affairs than the firm judgment—I hope very much the unanimous judgment—which I ask you to give in favour of the United Kingdom upon its claim.

These words also proved to be his final contribution to the case. A scandal back home in Britain demanded Sir Hartley's immediate recall to be at the service of the Lynskey Tribunal. Sir Frank Soskice, the Solicitor-General, was hurriedly called from London to take over from Sir Hartley and it fell to him to conduct Britain's case during the following six months. It was a task which would try his stamina and his patience to the utmost.

Days dragged into weeks as, one by one, Britain's witnesses were put before the Court. Captain Selby and Commander Paul relived their moments of anguish. Navigating officers were examined and cross-examined, on the courses they followed through the swept channel. Minesweeping experts told the story of the discovery of the minefield off Saranda Bay. All this evidence, important though it was to the proving of Britain's case, eventually became the mere predictable recital of known facts, relieved every now and then by the Albanian side trying to disprove a statement here and there.

The hearing really burst into life on the morning of 24 November, when the one man who could win or lose the case for either side was called before the court: Lieutenant Karel Kovacic, the Man from Sibenik. He was thirty-four years of age, but members of the British party at The Hague remember him as looking much older. The violent, and occasionally traumatic, course his life had taken had, it seemed, left its marks. And it was to some of these experiences that Sir Frank directed his early questions.

In the statement issued after Britain revealed the nature of

Kovacic's evidence, the Yugoslav Government tried desperately to undermine his credibility as a witness. He had, it was said, twice escaped from prisoner-of-war camps 'in suspicious circumstances'. And, for good measure, his wife 'had been sentenced to death for collaborating with the Gestapo'.

What, Sir Frank asked, was his answer to these charges? The clear suggestion that his story of escapes from prison camps was lies were met by Kovacic with a detailed story mentioning dates, and the names of men who had escaped with him. The first escape, he said, was from an Italian prisoner-of-war camp near Udine in June, 1942. With three friends he dug a tunnel under the camp into a field. They headed homewards, towards the Yugoslav border, but were captured a few days later by Italian troops. Kovacic was returned to the prison camp near Udine and spent twenty days' punishment in the cells for his pains.

In November of the same year he was transferred to a prisoner-of-war camp near Padua in Northern Italy. Ten months later, on 3 September, 1943, the Italians agreed an armistice with the Allies. In the resulting confusion—and before the Germans could take over the prison camp—Kovacic escaped once again. Two months later, having covered hundreds of miles on foot—a journey extended in both time and distance by the need to keep to unfrequented mountain roads and small villages to avoid recapture—Kovacic finally crossed both the German and Allied lines on the River Sangro in Central Italy and happily gave himself up to New Zealand troops.

Kovacic said he eventually rejoined the Royal Yugoslavian Navy and served with units of the British Fleet based on Malta. To the judges it must have seemed strange that a man who could endure such hardships and danger to escape captivity and to get involved in the war against the Germans should be labelled, in the ensuing peace, as a man who had escaped his captors 'under suspicious circumstances'.

Sir Frank then asked Kovacic to explain, as far as he could, the story that his wife had been executed as a Gestapo spy. To this allegation, a clear attempt by the Yugoslavs to smear him with his wife's purported collaboration, he replied that he knew nothing of the circumstances or of the evidence against her. How could he? At the time he was out of the country. And subsequent attempts to get at the truth had failed completely.

Sir Frank then switched Kovacic to the vital part of his evidence for the United Kingdom—his story of seeing mines loaded aboard the two Yugoslav ships in Sibenik four or five days before disaster struck the *Saumarez* and the *Volage*. He confirmed every word sworn in his affidavit in London. As Sir Frank sat down, having extracted all he wished from his witness, M Cot rose to his feet. And Karel Kovacic faced two days which, in retrospect, he acknowledged to be the most difficult in a life which had been full of affliction.

The Albanian Government could hardly have chosen a more formidable and forceful advocate to plead its case. Like his British opponents, Shawcross and Soskice, Pierre Cot was both lawyer and politician. From 1929 to 1940 he had represented Chambéry in the French Parliament, holding several ministerial posts, including Minister for Foreign Affairs (1932) and Minister of Aviation in several Cabinets between 1933 and 1937. He was a Radical Socialist and, in the eyes of the British team at The Hague, that meant Communist in all but name. Certainly he identified himself completely with Albania's case in a personal way which is unknown at the English Bar, where lawyers traditionally present a client's case factually and dispassionately, without ever appearing to allow their own views to intrude.

As a young man he studied at universities in Grenoble, his home town, and Paris. He was a doctor of law, a doctor of political science, and at the age of fifty-one, at the height of his intellectual powers. As a 'man of the mountains', as he sometimes described himself during the case, he professed to understand little of what happened in the world at sea level. But the witnesses who faced him at The Hague made their first mistake if they were deceived by this disarming confession. Senior officers and expert naval witnesses discovered that he had equipped himself to seize voraciously on any apparent discrepancy or inconsistency in their evidence.

Lawyers throughout the world always maintain that professional dichotomy, which frequently puzzles laymen, of being the best of friends and fierce court-room opponents at the same time. But, for once, Sir Hartley Shawcross found this attitude difficult to adopt. To him Pierre Cot was austere and aloof and only the briefest of civilities passed between them when they met in the robing room of the Court at the beginning and end of each session. Shawcross was also far from impressed by Cot's attitude to the case, which to the Attorney-General seemed to smack of a political crusade with David and Goliath overtones. Sir Frank Soskice, who had the benefit of a longer association with M Cot, found him an engaging man and they sometimes had long talks (on subjects unconnected with the Corfu Channel case, of course) over a glass of sherry or a meal after the day's court-room confrontations. But Sir Hartley and Sir Frank were in complete agreement on one issue—that M Cot was an opponent of considerable skill and intellect.

This then, was the man who, on the afternoon of 24 November, began his cross-examination of Karel Kovacic. M Cot's intention, made utterly clear by his opening questions, and eminently confirmed as his abrasive interrogation developed, was to pour such scorn on Kovacic's evidence as to destroy his credibility in the eyes of the judges. His attitude towards Kovacic during the long hours in which they faced each other was often hectoring, frequently sarcastic and at all times belligerent.

Was he aware that there were no such ships as *Mljet* and *Miljene* in the Yugoslav Navy? Kovacic, who answered all the questions in good English, gradually proved himself able to counter some of M Cot's so deviously phrased questions. It may well be there are no such ships as *Mljet* and *Miljene* in the Yugolsav Navy *now*, he said, because when the Communists took over they gave their ships initials and numbers. But the *Mljet* and the *Miljene* certainly existed when he was serving at Sibenik.

Later M Cot tried another similarly constructed question about the engineer-lieutenant who Kovacic said, had told him the two minesweepers had sailed on an important duty. Did Kovacic realize there was no such man bearing the name he had given in the Yugoslav Navy? Kovacic's reply was similarly wary. There may not be now, but there certainly was such a man in October 1946.

M Cot doubted that Kovacic could have seen any mines being loaded on the ships from the distance at which the launch passed Panakovic Cove—about 500 metres. Kovacic replied he certainly could; he remembered the late afternoon sun glistening on the dark paint on the mines, as though they had been newly painted.

M Cot even contrived to give Kovacic an eye-sight test in court. He produced a card on which two mines were drawn, but reduced in scale so that, at five metres' distance, they would appear as they did at 500 metres. He held the card five metres from Kovacic's eyes and asked him to tell him which of the drawings had a contact horn on it, and which did not.

Kovacic countered by saying it was unfair to give him such an eye-sight test because the light conditions in the courtroom were not as good as they had been out of doors at Sibenik. M Cot decided not to pursue his experimental eye-sight test.

M Cot tried to suggest that the angle of the sun's rays that evening were so low in the sky that they would not have given Kovacic sufficient light to see the mines so clearly at the times he stated. Kovacic was able to draw on his experience as a navigating officer to defend himself against the implications of that question. Yes, there was plenty of light; it was virtually broad daylight. And he was not prepared to accept M Cot's assessment of the angle of the sun's rays until he or other naval officers on the British side had checked it with the appropriate reference books and almanacs.

When Kovacic finally stepped from the witness box after his three long days, M Cot had been unable to shake him on any serious point. He was, for the British side, an excellent witness, giving his evidence calmly, and refusing to allow himself to be ruffled by M Cot's belligerent methods. His calmness, and the way in which he frequently detected the hidden motives in some of M Cot's questions and phrased his answers accordingly, drove the Frenchman to the point of obvious frustration. It was, perhaps, at these times that he realized he could not break down the Yugoslav and that, without doing so, he could not win the case.

As the hearing drew towards its close the Court decided to set up two committees of experts to advise the judges on two matters which were at the heart of the case, and on which the evidence as presented by both sides was in uncompromising conflict. The first committee was to go to Sibenik at once and re-trace Kovacic's motor boat journeys across the harbour to check on whether in fact he could have seen what he said he had seen. The second committee was ordered to go into Albania itself, back to the scene of the tragedy in the North Corfu Channel, to check on the look-out posts there and to answer the question: Could the Albanians have known mines were being laid so close to their shores?

All that remained now was to hear the final speeches from Soskice and Cot, and as the court was now approaching its twelfth week of continuous sittings, the fifteen judges were no doubt relieved to know their long incarceration was coming to an end.

Sir Frank's closing speech was a model of restrained, clinical, dispassionate advocacy. It summarized the evidence presented by both sides and, while it naturally came down heavily on recommending the court to accept the evidence of Britain's witnesses, it never to this end resorted to the wilder flights of exhortation. In fact Sir Frank's closing thoughts left with the judges, were not, as might be expected, a lofty peroration designed to sway any judge who might be wavering, and finally to convince any who were inclining towards accepting the British case. They were expressed in the form of a simple sum—the amount the British Government was claiming from Albania for the loss and damage it had sustained in the Corfu Channel two years and three months ago. It read like this:

Damage to H.M.S. *Saumarez*	£750,000
Damage to H.M.S. *Volage*	75,000
Compensation for the pensions and other expenses incurred by the Government of the United Kingdom in respect of the deaths and injuries of naval personnel.	50,000
	£875,000

Yet even this modest figure was not the final reckoning. It was found that the cost of fitting new bows to the *Volage* could be completed for £9,000 less than the original estimate. The claim was reduced accordingly.

Even the compensation due to the relatives was reduced because one or two had remarried. Britain indeed set against the bill the amount received from the sale of the *Saumarez* as scrap, a derisory and melancholy £4,000. The final bill worked out at £843,947 precisely.

Now it was the turn of M Cot, his last chance to win the case for Albania, a case in which he had become emotionally and politically involved to such an extent that more and more he was conducting it as a crusade of conscience rather than as a piece of detached advocacy. He poured withering scorn on Britain's insistence that her incursions into the Corfu Channel were utterly innocent. Time and again he quoted the now famous (or infamous) phrase about the Albanians learning to behave themselves. The whole affair, and the United Kingdom's subsequent attitude towards it, showed her to be adopting the traditional bullying role of a colonial power dealing with a weaker and near defenceless nation.

For nearly two days he held the attention of the judges—and the attention, plus the grudging admiration of his legal opponents—with a brilliant speech which was a fitting high point to a case that had dragged on for so long that it now moved into the January of 1949. But the end was in sight. The judges adjourned the court to go away to consider their verdict.

But, before that final moment, they had to consider the reports of the committees of experts who had been sent by the court to Saranda and Sibenik.

The committee ordered to Saranda inspected the Albanian coastal defences and look-out system. They reported back to the court that, if a proper look-out had been kept, it would have been impossible for the mines to have been laid as close to the shore as Operation Retail had proved, without the knowledge of the Albanians. The report from Sibenik was less clear-cut. The experts had stood in the same spot as that from which Kovacic said he clearly saw the two minelayers in Panakovic Cove, and the mines being loaded aboard them. They had tried to pick a day of similar weather conditions in order to make their observations as accurately as possible. They seemed agreed that a man standing at that spot would have been able to see ships in the cove. But they doubted whether anyone would be able to see the evening sunlight reflected on a mine.

After comments on these reports by both parties, the court returned to the awesome task of sifting through a mountain of documents and assessing enough words to fill a fair sized book-case—words which reflected all the bitterness and prevarication and contradiction to which the case had descended. It was a task which took them nearly three months.

On 9 April the court announced its findings. By eleven votes to five Albania was judged guilty of responsibility for the mining of the destroyers, and should pay compensation to Britain. The second issue before the court was whether Britain had violated international law when the destroyers were mined, and again in November, 1946, when the minesweepers were sent into the channel. By fourteen votes to two they decided Britain had not offended international law on the first occasion, but the judges were unanimous that the November activities of Operation Retail were a breach of Albania's sovereignty.

And so, almost three years after Captain Backa's ill-directed shell fire started the affair, it was ended. Britain's case was proved. Albania had been found guilty of an infamous crime.

As for the court's condemnation of the minesweeping operation, well, Britain could claim that without it—illegal though
the court had declared it to be—the mines would never have
been discovered and justice would never have been seen to be
done.

If Britain's legal advisers and the Foreign Office civil ser-
vants, wearily packing their bags thought that the end of the
case meant they could cast the weight of it from their shoulders,
they were soon to be disillusioned. In giving its judgment, the
court had granted Britain's claim for compensation in full. But
there was no provision for the court to enforce its judgment;
the aggrieved party was left to its own devices to collect its
own compensation. Very quickly the British Government realized that this would be no mere formality. Discussions between Sir Eric Beckett and a representative of the Albanian
Government began in Paris early in 1950. By the middle of
July the representatives of the two countries had met three
times. How, and when, do you propose to pay the money was
the question repeatedly put to the Albanians. The reply on
every occasion was: We do not have the money.

Some Members of Parliament began to show commendable
unease at the leisurely and unproductive manner in which these
negotiations were being conducted. Six days after that third
meeting the Under-Secretary of State for Foreign Affairs, Mr
Ernest Davies, was asked in the House to report on the progress, if any, which was being made at the Paris meetings. His
reply revealed a quite amazing naivety. He said:

> A third discussion took place in Paris on 17 July. It
> was inconclusive, but the Albanian delegate was pressed
> hard to put forward concrete proposals. He was told that
> failure to do so would compel His Majesty's Government
> *to doubt the Albanian Government's good faith.* It is
> expected that a further meeting will take place shortly.

While allowance must be made for the traditional niceties
of diplomatic language, to refer, after all that had gone before,
to Albanian good faith leaves one with the clear impression

that the Government was not pursuing the claim in the most positive way. Many MPs had the distinct impression that, having won the battle at The Hague, the Government was not prepared to invest mere debt collection with the same overtones of morality.

The infrequent and desultory meetings continued in Paris. They served only to provide further proof of Albania's utter intransigence.

In March, 1951, a Conservative back bencher, Mr Boyd-Carpenter, raised the matter in the Commons. 'It seems quite intolerable,' he declared, 'that the matter should be allowed to rest where it now lies. Not only was the incident in the Corfu Channel a quite intolerable affront to the dignity and to the prestige of the Royal Navy and this country, it was equally an act of plain murder committed on behalf of the Albanian Government.' If, as seemed clear, the Albanian Government would not pay the compensation willingly, it was the British Government's duty to force payment from them. Were there no Albanian assets in Britain or the Empire which could be seized in lieu of payment? Had the Government even considered such a course?

Mr Davies replied that the Government had indeed considered the question of assets. Unfortunately Albania had no assets in Britain's sphere of influence. And even if they had, he felt it would be an 'extremely serious step to obtain possession of the property of a sovereign power in time of peace'. Some MPs no doubt felt that this respect for the sanctity of Albanian property would hardly impress the relatives of the forty-four men who died because of Albania's contempt of other people's property and lives.

Mr Boyd-Carpenter persisted. Were there no Albanian ships which could be seized?

The only Albanian ships known to the Government were small fishing vessels in the Mediterranean and it was not felt worth while to seize them on the high seas. Mr Davies urged the MPs to consider how difficult it was to extract payment from a country which literally refused to pay. There was no record of any trade between Britain and Albania, so sanctions in that direction were impossible. He ended his defence of the Government's conduct with a statement, with which no one could disagree, about the relatives who had lost sons and husbands aboard the two destroyers. He said, 'Theirs is a tragedy greater than failure to obtain monetary satisfaction.'

The significant factor about this debate is not in what was said; the words on either side of the House were predictable. The significance lies in the time the debate was held and the amount of time allotted to it. It began at 2.16 *a.m.* and, under the rules of the House was restricted to a duration of thirty minutes only. It ended at 2.46 a.m. precisely, with one MP's question unanswered by the minister. Only a handful of MPs were present for a debate initiated by a back-bencher; the Government, in the midst of post-war problems it judged to be more pressing, could find no Parliamentary time to debate the affair. Some observers will judge that the Government had no real desire to find the time for a discussion which would expose its failure to extract from Albania the penalties imposed by the International Court.

There remained only one more hope of collecting the compensation. It was discovered that, although Albania had few tangible assets outside the borders of her own country, there was a sum of money ready to be seized, and it was in gold. This gold was part of a loan made over to Albania by the Italians before the war. When, towards the end of the war, the Germans began to flee from Albania, they took the gold with them. It was added to other stocks of looted gold amounting to no less than 350 tons, worth at least £140,000,000 at the post-war rates. It was hidden in various places in Austria and Germany; the biggest haul was found by the Allies in a salt mine in Austria. More looted gold had been sent to neutral countries to be stored for the Nazis or had been handed over to neutrals in payment for food and supplies sent to Germany.

A Tripartite Commission made up of Britain, France and the United States was set up to tackle the formidable task of hearing Governments' claims and apportioning the return of the gold to the rightful owners. It was a task which took twenty years. Albania claimed the £600,000 as her own. Italy put in a counter claim, saying that the gold was part of the Italian loan to Albania which was never repaid. And Britain said the gold should be *hers* in part settlement of the compensation. Britain again found herself before the International Court, which had been asked to decide to whom the gold should go. And so began another saga years long before the court finally came to a decision—that it was not competent to give a decision. It was left to Britain and Italy to decide among themselves who should have the gold. And, ironically, the spoils of war on this occasion went to the vanquished; the victor got nothing.

Albania's compensation to Britain has never been paid. Hopes that it might be have long since been abandoned. The amount has been written off; a mere drop in the financial ocean of post-war debts. Albania has, as Mr Boyd-Carpenter and other people feared, got away with murder.

But to some people the bigger *débâcle* is at The Hague. In the Corfu Channel case the court attempted to establish its authority and its ability to solve international disputes. The failure to invest it with the authority to enforce its decisions led to its eventual impotency.

Little now remains to remind us of one of the cruellest and most inglorious incidents in the history of the Royal Navy. Not the ships. *Mauritius* and *Leander* and brave *Saumarez* have long since gone to the Valhalla which those of plebeian minds call the breakers' yards. Only *Volage* remains intact. In her quiet old age, she was eventually retired to a grace and favour life in Portsmouth harbour as a training ship for Royal Marines. She is now waiting for her voyage to the breakers' yard.

And very few of the men remain. The senior officers of 1946 have, like their ships, retired. The young seamen and stokers and signalmen are now teachers, bus drivers, miners, clerks. They are married and have teenage children of their own. One or two are grandfathers. Karel Kovacic has vanished as mysteriously as he arrived. At the end of the hearings at The Hague he left Europe, ostensibly for South America. He has not been heard of since.

Albania remains as ever it was . . . enigmatic, suspicions, still withdrawn behind the barriers of its own introspection. Occasionally Comrade Hoxha, still in command, sanctions a slight relaxation and the borders are opened to brief and carefully observed visits by tourists. And then, without warning, even this small chink in the curtain is hurriedly closed, as though so slight a contact with the outside world would lead to contamination.* The Albanian peasant remains as he has always been—very poor and utterly dominated.

Ships of all nations now pass through the Corfu Channel. Once the two war-time mine-fields guarding the northern approach were swept, vessels no longer had to sail close to the Albanian shore, and Comrade Hoxha and his men abandoned the prickly sensitivity which led to the tragedies of 1946.

A quarter of a century has transformed the island of Corfu. It is now the holiday paradise which travel agents and those phenomena of the post-war years, the package-tour operators, love to 'discover'. Huge jet airliners (carefully avoiding Albanian air space) swoop down on the sickle-shaped patch of green nestling in its sea of blue and disgorge their streams of holiday-makers. For them Corfu means no more than golden beaches, dark-watered mysterious inlets, lobster fishing, traditional Greek songs in a taverna.

The harbour where once *Saumarez* lay, broken and burning,

---

* A senior executive of a British national newspaper recently discovered to what lengths the Albanians are prepared to go to shield themselves from what they call 'Western decadent influences'. While on holiday in Yugoslavia the border with Albania was opened and he joined a one-day coach trip into the country. During lunch in a town just across the border he was approached by a policeman and told that he could not stay in the country unless he had his sideboards shortened. He refused to do so, saying they were not over-long by any reasonable standard. The policeman insisted that if he continued to refuse to he would be taken to the border and put across it. Not wishing to be parted from his wife, and from the coach which was his only means of returning to his holiday resort in Yugoslavia, he had to agree. He was escorted from the restaurant to a barber's shop and the offending sideboards were trimmed by about an inch.

and *Volage* showed her scars, is now filled with the shipping of peace and affluence. White cruise liners nod gracefully at their anchors. Sailing boats wheel and turn between the yachts of the wealthy of the Western world. The ubiquitous caiques which link Corfu with the nearby islands chug-chug-chug steadily along their ordered courses.

And even less remains to mock the conscience of a nation which cared too little and forgot too quickly. Just twelve white crosses in a Corfu cemetery and, for Petty Officer Zarb, a lonely grave in Malta.

For the thirty-one other men who vanished in the explosions, or whose bodies could not be identified, there is not even that final dignity.

They, like thousands of sailors before them, have no known grave but the sea.

Epilogue

*On 4 April, 1972, the following letter was sent
to the Albanian Ambassador in Paris.*

Your Excellency,

I am researching a book about an incident in the Corfu
Channel in 1946 when two British destroyers struck mines with
a severe loss of life to the crews.

As I am sure you are aware, this matter eventually was
decided upon by the International Court of Justice at the Hague
and compensation was awarded to the British Government
against the Government of Albania. This compensation has
not been paid.

It is my earnest desire that the book on which I am working
shall be utterly fair in all respects and will reflect the views of
both countries involved. To that end I would be obliged if
you would ask your Government in Tirana to give me, with
a view to inclusion in the book, a statement expressing the
Government's opinion.

Yours sincerely,
Eric Leggett
36, The Mead
Beckenham
Kent

There was no reply.

APPENDIX I

The Men Who Died

H.M. Destroyer *Saumarez* (mined not sunk 22 October, 1946)

Killed

BRIFFA Victor E D, *Assistant Steward*	E/LX 667166
MORRIS Ronald, *Cook*	D/MX 750902
WINTER Brian J, *Leading Radio Mechanic*	P/MX 742378
WINTERBOTTOM Sam, *Able Seaman*	D/SSX 729949

Died of injuries

		Date of death
BEVAN Leslie Oliver, *Stoker 1st Class*	D/KX 98551	24 Oct.
De BATTISTA Antonio, *Leading Steward*	E/LX 23209	23 Oct.
EVA Stanley John, *Leading Cook*	D/MX 53041	22 Oct.
HALES Gordon Henry, *Able Seaman*	D/JX 652361	23 Oct.
SAYERS William H, *Acting Leading Stoker*	D/SKX 86	23 Oct.
WEAVER John, *Leading Seaman*	D/JX 150227	24 Oct.
ZARB Salvatore, *PO Cook*	E/LX 20225	4 Nov.

Missing presumed killed

ATKINSON Bernard, *Leading Radio Mechanic*	C/MX 65847
BECKETT Launston B, *Cook*	D/MX 750559
BUTCHER Donald George, *Stoker 2nd Class*	C/KX 779246
EDWARDS William A D, *Writer*	C/MX738317
FISHER Robert, *Acting Able Seaman*	D/JX 655048
FORD William J N, *ERA 5th Class*	D/MX 93556
FRANCIS Vernon, *Able Seaman*	D/JX 709105
GALLAHAR Enoch J, *Telegraphist*	D/JX 724465
GERMAN Raymond, *Able Seaman (Radar)*	D/JX 708935
GOODE Trevor W, *Stoker 2nd Class*	P/KX 763125
HALL Francis R, *Telegraphist*	D/JX 711742
HOLMES Norman, *Able Seaman*	D/JX 642544
KITT William J H, *Acting Leading Stoker*	D/KX 98204
LEWIS John, *Able Seaman*	P/JX 632719
LLEWELLYN Frederick E, *Able Seaman*	D/JX 679885
LOCK Samuel, *Stores Petty Officer*	P/MX 59959
MALLIA Francis X, *Assistant Cook*	E/MX 777962
MUNN Reginald H, *Petty Officer Writer*	D/MX 58072
PARSONS Ernest William, *Chief Petty Officer*	D/JX 125562
PINE William H, *Stoker Petty Officer*	D/KX 90676

ROSS William P J, *Acting Able Seaman*   D/JX 650092
SCHOLES Frank M, *C.P.O. Telegraphist*   D/J 112746
SPEIGHT Gordon, *Ord. Telegraphist*   P/JX 745538
STAERCK Walter John, *Able Seaman*   D/JX 709285
WILSON Henry J R T, *Acting Leading
Telegraphist*   D/JX 245788

H.M. Destroyer *Volage* (mined not sunk 22 October, 1946)

OFFICERS

Missing presumed killed
Sub-Lieutenant (E) H G Price, RNVR

RATINGS

Killed
KNOTT Joseph, *Petty Officer*   P/JX 161869

Missing presumed killed
BROOM Harry G, *Leading Stoker*   P/KX 92073
CHANNELL Archibald J, *Stoker Petty Officer*   P/KX 88770
LOCHLIN James L A, *Stoker 2nd Class*   D/KX 786732
MILLSON William E, *E.R.A. 3rd Class*   P/MX 55187
TAYLOR Cyril J, *Stoker 2nd Class*   P/KX 784766

Died of injuries
KEETON Cyril, *Stoker Petty Officer*   P/KX 78483

APPENDIX II

This report by Captain Selby of the incidents of 22 October was written the following day when his ship had returned to Corfu. It was addressed to the President of the Board of Inquiry which had been set up by the Commander-in-Chief, Mediterranean, to investigate the circumstances of the mining of the two destroyers.

Report of Captain Selby, 23 October, 1946.
H.M.S. *Saumarez*, At Corfu.

Destroyers left harbour an hour before cruisers in order to prepare for action in accordance with the orders laid down in XCU issued by Rear-Admiral First Cruiser Squadron.

At 13.30 *Saumarez* took station 2½ cables astern of *Mauritius* ... and proceeded at ten knots through the swept Channel.

At 1447 off Ford Edda course was altered to 310 deg. by Red turn from the Rear-Admiral 1st Cruiser Squadron; the ship was in station astern when at 1453 a heavy explosion occurred underneath the forepart of the bridge accompanied by a large brilliant yellow flash on the port side and another shooting outward through the starboard side. The ship lost steam immediately and began to settle by the bows. Telegraphs were put to Stop as soon as possible and as soon as smoke had cleared preliminary investigation showed a considerable area of damage below water from the funnel to abreast 'B' gun. Smoke and flame soon appeared and the bridge was evacuated for the emergency conning position. Steam was again raised in No. 2 boiler within a very short time but reports received showed a major fire in the vicinity of the for'ard oil fuel tanks and for'ard Bofors magazine and shell rooms.

The starboard side of the hull abreast the bridge has been blown out. No. 1 boiler room immediately flooded as did probably all compartments as far forward as the fore end of the stokers mess deck. Dense clouds of smoke and considerable flame were coming from the region of the W/T Office and a ring of flame appeared close to the starboard side of the ship forward; this spread and set fire a large amount of oil fuel floating near the starboard bow.

About this time pressure became available on the after section of the fire main and fire-fighting commenced from the break of the foc'sle. Inspection showed that the flat containing the T.S. W/T Office, radar and other offices was a raging inferno, which accounted for the large number of casualties.

The ship had been falling off the wind all the time, and luckily drifted off the fuel burning on the surface: the internal fires were, however, obviously being fed from what fuel remained under the ship. The fire was attacked from both fore and aft, whilst a check was being made whether the ship could be steamed stern-first. The ship had drifted out of the swept channel towards the lee shore of Albania, and preparations were made for being taken in tow aft by H.M.S. *Volage*, who was then closing.

At this time engines were reported ready for trial and the ship was manoeuvred by engines to turn stern to wind whilst *Volage* closed and towed *Saumarez* stern first. Considerable trouble in keeping steam was experienced due, as proved later, to sea water leaking into the feed line to No. 2 boiler.

As the ship was towing comfortably, every effort was made to combat the fire with hoses and foam available, whilst casualties were collected abreast the after tubes for attention.

It appeared that the fire was being confined to the original area, but at approximately 1630 *Volage* was seen to have her bows blown off and she slipped the tow. This was left on *Saumarez* towing slip in the hope that it would assist in keeping the stern up to wind, but owing to the depth of water no value was obtained.

At approximately 1600 main engines were again moved and ship was turned stern to wind, after which steam failed again completely, as the boiler primed due to the salt water in the feed system.

This left the ship with no power of any kind, as the after diesel was defective and the foremost was in No. 1 boiler room. The fires therefore spread rapidly and took a firm hold, as the only fire appliances available were two hand pumps.

An excellent piece of ship-handling by *Volage* resulted in her again taking *Saumarez* in tow bow to stern and proceeding stern first south through the swept channel to Corfu.

An interval of some two-and-a-half hours elapsed before an emergency lead could be run from *Volage* and pumps and lights supplied; after which fire-fighting continued from the break of the foc'sle and the bridge, and ready use ammunition at 'A' and 'B' guns was then thrown overboard except for a few rounds at the former which were unapproachable due to heat.

As the for'ard bulkhead of No. 2 boiler room was intact except for a small leak through an electric gland, I decided that the ship could well be got to Corfu, although probably the forepart would have to burn itself out assisted by the moderate wind from astern. *Mauritius* boat arrived at dusk wth portable diesel pump and medical assistance, both of which were invaluable.

At approximately 2030 *Raider* joined and was asked to close the starboard bow of *Saumarez* and endeavour to cool the ship's side from outboard. Excellent ship-handling by the Commanding Officer for three or more hours kept *Raider* close enough to be of great value in this. From 2100 cruisers and *Ocean's* boats arrived, transporting casualties to shore and *Ocean* fetching fire-fighting stores, etc., whilst *Ocean* provided a strong fire-fighting team with foam who, by working in shifts, finally got the fire under control. *Volage* and *Saumarez* secured astern of *Leander* for the night on arrival.

All remaining casualties were then evacuated to *Ocean* and the majority of the ship's company followed for the night, leaving 4 officers and approximately 30 ratings on board.

Before securing the foremost bulkhead of No. 2 boiler room was shored up with assistance from *Leander*, as by this time the boiler was cool enough to work around, and the ship had settled more by the bow.

The following morning the Rear-Admiral 1st Cruiser Squadron and later the Commander-in-Chief Mediterranean visited *Saumarez*, by which time all fires were well under control and arrangements were made to tow both ships to a smoother anchorage to await the arrival of *Ranpura*.

All times given above are of necessity approximate only, and may in some cases be considerably in error owing to the difficulties of estimating time correctly under such circumstances.

A list of suggested witnesses is enclosed.

I have the honour to be, Sir,
Your obedient servant,
(signed) W. H. Selby,
Captain (D).

The President of the Board (three copies).

Copies to: The Commander-in-Chief, Mediterranean (afloat).
The Rear-Admiral 1st Cruiser Squadron
The Commanding Officer, H.M. Ship *Volage*.

Encl.—List of suggested witnesses.

APPENDIX III

The following complete histories of the four ships involved in The Corfu Incident were kindly supplied by the Historical Branch of the Royal Navy.

H.M.S. SAUMAREZ
Summary of Service

H.M.S. *Saumarez* was a Fleet destroyer, 'S' class, built by Hawthorn Leslie, Hebburn, Newcastle upon Tyne, and completed on 1 July, 1943. Her standard displacement was 1,730 tons, length 363 feet, breadth 35 feet, mean draught 14 feet and armament, four 4.7-inch single, one Bofors twin and four Oerlikon twin power.

After working up, *Saumarez* was allocated to the 3rd Destroyer Flotilla, Home Fleet, and shortly after to the 23rd Destroyer Flotilla. She was one of the escorts which sailed from Seidisfiord on 23 October taking with them five Russian minesweepers and six Russian motor launches to bring back from the Kola Inlet thirteen ships which had been there since the spring. The convoy (RA 54A) sailed from Archangel on 1 November as it had been delayed by the thick fog.

The *Saumarez* escorted an outgoing Arctic convoy shortly afterwards, which also arrived without loss or damage. On 22 December convoy RA 55A sailed from Kola, escorted by eight destroyers, including H.M.S. *Saumarez*, two Canadian destroyers, three corvettes and a minesweeper. The outgoing convoy, JW 55B, had left Loch Ewe on 20 December and was expected to reach Bear Island on Christmas Day about the same time as RA 55A. Cruiser cover was provided east of Bear Island by the *Belfast*, *Sheffield* and *Norfolk*, and heavy cover by the battleship *Duke of York*.

Early on 26 December the Admiralty signalled that the German battle cruiser *Scharnhorst* was at sea. She was detected by the cruisers and after some hours trying to evade them and strike at the convoy, headed for home. She was intercepted and hit by the *Duke of York* and a long chase followed.

In the ensuing action, the *Saumarez*'s guns fired continuously for eleven minutes, followed by torpedo attacks. A shell from the *Scharnhorst* which did not explode passed through the Director Control Tower, killing three men and putting the tower out of action. A near miss also damaged the forced lubrication system.

The *Scharnhorst* was sunk, three hours after the first sighting, by the *Duke of York* and the cruisers. The four destroyers, *Saumarez, Savage, Scorpion* and *Stord* had scored at least three hits. H.M.S. *Saumarez* steamed to Murmansk on one engine and after temporary repairs by the Russians left for the U.K.

Following a refit, completed in March, 1944, she was again part of the escort of a pair of Arctic convoys, JW 58 and RA 58, both of which reached their destinations unscathed. The successful Fleet Air Arm attack on the German battleship *Tirpitz*, which took place on 3 April, was synchronized with the passage of JW 58.

In Operation 'Neptune', the landings in Normandy in June, 1944 H.M.S. *Saumarez* was Senior Officer's ship of the 23rd Destroyer Flotilla which gave gun support to Force S in the assault on Ouistreham. The *Saumarez* and the destroyer *Onslaught* engaged a convoy of three or four minesweepers and one merchant vessel off St Peter Port, Guernsey on 14 August.

The convoy was frequently hit but both destroyers sustained slight damage and a few casualties. In September the *Saumarez* was part of the escort of another Arctic convoy. She was refitted at Newcastle from November to January, 1945, prior to joining the 26th Destroyer Flotilla, East Indies Fleet.

Early in January, 1945, the *Saumarez* left the Clyde to rendezvous with the carrier *Formidable* and escort her from Alexandria to Colombo. She arrived at Colombo on 8 February and Trincomalee on 10 March. On 14 March the *Saumarez* took part in a sweep in the Andaman Sea, with the destroyers *Volage* and *Rapid*. They found and destroyed a junk in Stewart Sound, but *Rapid* and *Volage* sustained damage and casualties from hits from a coastal gun, reported to be 6 inch or larger. On 25 March, a further sweep was made. A Japanese convoy was sighted the next day and engaged. Although the destroyers attacked with gunfire and torpedoes they made few hits, and being low on ammunition, called on two Liberator aircraft to sink the enemy. One of these sank one of the Japanese auxiliaries *Risui Maru* with bombs. The *Volage* sank the other auxiliary, *Teshio Maru*, with gunfire. Both escorts were also sunk.

H.M.S. *Saumarez* was in Force 63 in April, when she bombarded Oleelhoe, Sumatra. She was part of the Carrier Force in Operation 'Bishop', formed to protect the convoys in the seaborne assault on Rangoon, and then took part in Operation 'Dukedom', which was mounted to attack the Japanese force reported to be sailing from Singapore on 10 May.

On this occasion, she was part of the newly constituted Force 61. The Japanese cruiser *Haguro* and destroyer *Kamikaze* had left Malacca Strait on 14 May and early next day an Avenger operating from the Assault Carrier *Emperor* sighted them. The *Saumarez*, *Verulam* and *Vigilant* in one division and the *Venus* and *Virago* in a second, were diverted to intercept. Both ships were attacked by the destroyers early on 16 May. The *Haguro*, overwhelmed by their torpedoes, went to the bottom at 0209 in a position some forty-five miles south-west of Penang. The *Kamikaze* was damaged but managed to escape.

H.M.S. *Saumarez* was refitted at Durban from June to August. Although Japan had formally surrendered on 2 September, the occupation of Western Malaya (Operation 'Zipper') was carried out almost as planned originally. H.M.S. *Saumarez* was one of the fifteen destroyers screening the operation. The 26th Destroyer Flotilla left the East Indies Headquarters at Colombo on 17 November and arrived in the U.K. early in December. The *Saumarez* went to Plymouth for refit and preparation for service in the Mediterranean.

Early in March, 1946 the *Saumarez* sailed for the Mediterranean, for service in the 3rd Destroyer Flotilla. In June she intercepted a caique carrying 382 illegal emigrants bound for Palestine and towed the caique to Haifa. A boarding party from the *Saumarez* also arrested S.S. *Hochelaga* off Haifa on 31 July, carrying 500 emigrants. On 26 September *Saumarez* sailed on a Mediterranean cruise with twenty-four other ships. Orders were given for a part of the 1st Cruiser Squadron to pass from South to North of the Corfu Strait.

On 22 October the *Saumarez*, preceded by the cruiser *Mauritius*, and with the cruiser *Leander* and the *Volage* set course to proceed through the swept Medri Channel. The *Saumarez* struck a mine at 1453, which caused severe damage and casualties. The *Volage* closed her to take her in tow and after some difficulty, managed to pass the tow and began to tow the *Saumarez* stern first. At 1606 however, a mine exploded near the *Volage*, wrecking the ship forward. She was able to re-connect the tow to the *Saumarez*, and the two destroyers, both stern-first, reached the Corfu Roads at 0310 on 23 October. The *Saumarez* was moved to Malta, where she remained until September, 1950, when she was towed back to the U.K. and broken up at Rosyth.

H.M.S. *Saumarez* was awarded the following Battle Honours:

North Cape	1943
Arctic	1943–44
Normandy	1944
Malaya	1945
Burma	1945

H.M.S. VOLAGE
Summary of Service

H.M.S. *Volage*, a Fleet destroyer of the Valentine (or V) class, was built by J. S. White & Co. Limited, Cowes, Isle of Wight, and completed 26 May, 1944: standard displacement 1,710 tons, length 363 feet, breadth 36 feet and mean draught 14 feet, and armament four 4.7-inch single four twin-power pom-poms and eight 20 mm Oerlikons.

After working up at Scapa, she was allocated to the 26th Destroyer Flotilla, Home Fleet. In August, the success of the Normandy invasion appearing assured, convoys to North Russia were resumed, and an operation ('Goodwood') was mounted, with the aim of putting out of action the German battleship *Tirpitz*, lying at Altenfiord, in order to safeguard the convoys. This operation by carrier-borne aircraft was synchronized with the running of the convoy, which left Loch Ewe on 15 August, and the *Volage* was one of the destroyers in the strong force which also served as heavy cover for the convoy. Although strikes were made on three occasions, when the weather permitted flying, the results were disappointing. A heavy smoke screen forced the fighters to bomb blind and bombers did not reach the target owing to poor weather, but many other vessels and subsidiary shore targets were damaged.

The *Volage* escorted two Arctic convoys in September and October, JW 60 which left Loch Ewe on 15 September and RA 60, which left Russia on 28 September. The first accomplished the passage safely, but two merchant ships were lost to U boats in RA 60. In October another air strike was made on shipping in Norwegian waters by aircraft from the carrier *Implacable*. Six destroyers of the 26th Destroyer Flotilla escorted *Implacable* and the cruiser *Mauritius*, and the attacks were highly successful. In November the 26th Destroyer Flotilla was allocated for the Eastern Theatre and the *Volage* was taken in hand for essential defects and docking. She left Gourock on 11 January, 1945 for the East Indies Station, and arrived at Trincomalee on 10 February.

H.M.S. *Volage* took part in three operations in February and March, 1945. The first, Operation 'Stacey', when she was in Force 62, was a photographic reconnaissance off the coast of Malaya. The second was Operation 'Transport' in the Andaman Sea when, with *Saumarez* and *Rapid* comprising Force 70, she bombarded Port Blair, and destroyed a junk in Stewart Sound, but came under fire from the shore defences and was hit, losing three men.

The third, Operation 'Onboard', comprised a further sweep in the Andaman Sea, where a Japanese convoy of two naval auxiliaries escorted by two submarine chasers was sighted. *Volage* fired four torpedoes at the larger auxiliary, the *Risui Maru*, but these missed; she eventually sank the smaller one, the *Teshio Maru* with gunfire. A Liberator sank the *Risui Maru*, and both escorts were sunk. H.M.S. *Volage* went to Durban for a refit early in April, returning to Colombo on 6 August. Following the Japanese surrender, *Volage* took part in the operation to occupy Penang. Six forces, under the command of the Flag Officer Commanding the 3rd Battle Squadron, with his flag in H.M.S. *Nelson*, left Trincomalee on 17 August. On 28 August, senior Japanese officers came on board the *Nelson* and the *London* to sign undertakings that no attack would be made on the Fleet. The surrender was formally signed on 2 September and the port occupied by Royal

Marines. The *Volage* remained at Penang for wireless purposes until a shore station was available. The 26th Destroyer Flotilla left Colombo for the U.K. on 17 November: the *Volage* arrived at Portsmouth early in December to begin a refit in preparation for service in the Mediterranean .

H.M.S. *Volage* left the U.K. early in March, 1946 for the Mediterranean and service with the 3rd Destroyer Flotilla. Towards the end of May the *Volage*, *Saumarez* and *Venus*, with drafts embarked, sailed to Haifa to relieve the 14th Destroyer Flotilla. On 13 August the *Volage* arrested the *Katdiel-Goffe*, carrying illegal emigrants to Palestine. She sailed on 26 September, with twenty-four other ships, for a Mediterranean Fleet cruise.

Part of the 1st Cruiser Squadron was ordered to pass from South to North of the Corfu Strait. The Cruiser *Mauritius*, followed by the *Saumarez* and the cruiser *Leander* followed by the *Volage*, set course to proceed through the swept Medri Channel on 22 October. At 1453 the *Saumarez* struck a mine, suffering severe damage and casualties. The *Volage* was ordered to close her, take her in tow and return with her to Corfu Roads. This was accomplished, although *Volage* had her bows blown off by another mine.

The *Volage* was refitted at Malta, completing in August, 1947, and served in the Mediterranean until May, 1949, when she returned to Portsmouth and following a refit, reduced to Reserve. Her conversion to A/S Frigate began early in 1951 and was completed in October, 1953. In November she joined the 3rd Training Squadron, Plymouth Command, based at Londonderry. The *Volage* was employed on a search off Northern Ireland for a missing Shackleton of Coastal Command in December. Wreckage was found in Scallacastle Bay. In June, 1954, with the frigate *Relentless*, she visited Amsterdam. She was refitted at Rosyth between February and April, 1955 and in June of that year visited St Jean de Luz. In March, 1956 she began to reduce to Operational Reserve, and she remained in Reserve at Portsmouth until March, 1966, when it was decided that she should not be disposed of, but employed at Portsmouth as a Harbour Training Ship for the Royal Marines. She is currently on the Disposal List.

H.M.S. *Volage* was awarded the following Battle Honour:

Arctic 1944.

H.M.S. MAURITIUS
Summary of Service

H.M.S. *Mauritius* was a 6-inch cruiser of the 'Fiji' type and was authorized in the Navy Estimates of 1937–38. She was built by Swan Hunter and Wigham Richardson on the Tyne and engined by the Wallsend Slipway and Engineering Company. Laid down on 31 March, 1938, she was launched on 19 July, 1939, and completed on 1 January, 1941. Her standard displacement was 8,000 tons, and she had an extreme length of 555½ feet, extreme breadth of 62 feet and mean draught of 16½ feet. She was originally armed with twelve 6-inch guns in four triple turrets. Geared turbines of 65,000 horse power driving four shafts gave her a designed speed of 31½ knots. She had one Walrus aircraft.

The *Mauritius* joined the 10th Cruiser Squadron, Home Fleet, on 7 January, 1941, at Scapa, but from mid-February was detached to escort the troop convoy WS 6B on the first stage of its voyage to the Middle East, arriving at Freetown on 5 March. A week later she left escorting the Sierra Leone convoy SL 68 en route to the United Kingdom. Later in the month after fuelling at Bathurst, she rendered similar service to convoy SL 69. In April she escorted convoys SL 71, and in May another Middle East troop convoy, WS 8A, to the Cape. She was then ordered to relieve the *Shropshire* on the East Indies Station, and did so on 20 June, arriving at Mombasa on the 27th, after escorting CM 11 to Aden.

On 6 November she arrived at Singapore with convoy WS 11X. A month later, after the entry of Japan into the war, the *Mauritius* was allocated to the Eastern Fleet, but returned to the United Kingdom for refit. She arrived at Plymouth on 11 February, 1942, and was under refit at Devonport until April. After working up at Scapa she arrived in the Clyde on 9 May and left next day escorting a troop convoy, WS 19. She left Simonstown on 10 June escorting this convoy, and was employed on escort and patrol duties in the Eastern Fleet until 1943.

In February, 1943, the *Mauritius* was among the ships which provided cover in the Indian Ocean to the return of the 9th Australian Division from Suez to Australia in five large transports. When a 6-inch cruiser was required from the Eastern Fleet to take part in the landing in Sicily, the *Mauritius* was selected, and eventually left Kilindini on 29 May for Aden, Suez and Port Said, joining the 15th Cruiser Squadron on her arrival in the Mediterranean.

In the Sicily landing on 10 July, Operation 'Husky', the *Mauritius* took part in various bombardments as a unit of the Support Force under Rear-Admiral C. H. J. Harcourt. After the *Newfoundland* was torpedoed by a U-boat on 23 July, Rear-Admiral Harcourt transferred his flag to the *Mauritius*. She was thus employed in later operations in Italy, including the landing near Reggio (Operation 'Baytown') on 3 September, and the landing at Salerno (Operation 'Avalanche') on 9 September. The supporting squadron remained in the northern assault area until 5 October, when the *Mauritius* and other ships left for Naples.

On 24 December the *Mauritius* was detailed for Operation 'Stonewall', the interception of enemy blockade runners in the Bay of Biscay, after which she was detached to Plymouth, arriving there on 2 January, 1944. She left a week later to return to the Mediterranean.

On 24 January, 1944, the *Mauritius* joined in the bombardments connected with Operation 'Shingle', the landing at Anzio two days earlier. Gun support was continued at intervals until March.

On 2 April, the *Mauritius* left Gibraltar and the Mediterranean Station for England to prepare to take part in the Normandy landing, and was repaired at Chatham until May. She was allocated to the 1st Cruiser Squadron, Home Fleet. In the landing, Operation 'Neptune', she flew the flag of Rear-Admiral W. R. Patterson, Commanding the Second Cruiser Squadron, allocated to Bombardment Force D in the Eastern Task Force under Rear-Admiral Sir Philip Vian.

The *Mauritius* was the only big ship to take part in the four invasions of Sicily, Salerno, Anzio and Normandy and under the command of Captain W. W. Davis she bombarded the enemy on over 250 occasions.

The flag of Rear-Admiral Patterson was struck on 21 June, but the *Mauritius* continued in the Bombarding Squadron during July. In August she was transferred to operations in the Bay of Biscay. On the 15th with two destroyers, she severely handled an enemy convoy between Sables d'Olonne and La Pallice consisting of a destroyer, two M-class minesweepers, four merchant vessels and a small tanker. A further success was obtained on 23 August, in Audierne Bay, when two M-class minesweepers, three flak ships, one medium and two small merchant ships were destroyed.

The *Mauritius* was under repair at Plymouth during September, and on 17 October arrived at Scapa to rejoin the Home Fleet. A week later she left with a force from that Fleet which attacked enemy shipping in the Norwegian Leads, Operation 'Athletic', between 26 and 28, by air strikes from the carrier *Implacable*, in which the C-in-C, Home Fleet, flew his flag.

On 20 December, the *Mauritius* was with another force of the Home Fleet which left Scapa under the Vice-Admiral, 10th Cruiser Squadron, to attack enemy shipping off Norway near Aaalesund. No shipping was sighted, however, and the force returned on the 23rd.

On 27 January, 1945, the cruisers *Diadem*, flagship of the Vice-Admiral, 10th Cruiser Squadron, and *Mauritius* left Scapa to intercept three German destroyers of the 'Narvik' class reported off Norway. Interception took place early next morning about fifty miles north-west of Bergen. In an inconclusive action at high speed, during which the enemy made continuous smoke, the *Mauritius* had one man wounded from one shell-hit by a destroyer.

On 23 February the *Mauritius* left Scapa for Birkenhead, where she was under refit until March, 1946. She left a month later to relieve the *Sirius* in the Mediterranean, arriving at Malta on 26 April. In June, the flag of the F.O., 15th Cruiser Squadron, was transferred to her from the *Orion*. This squadron was shortly afterwards renumbered the 1st Cruiser Squadron.*

On 19 April, 1948, the flag of the Rear-Admiral was transferred to the *Phoebe* and the *Mauritius* arrived at Portsmouth on the 30th. She was under refit for a year, and on 6 May, 1949, left Devonport for the East Indies Station to replace the *Norfolk*.

Between 9 and 19 September, 1950, the *Mauritius* visited the Island of Mauritius after which she was named.

For much of 1951 the *Mauritius* was employed in the Persian Gulf, where the oilfields at Abadan were nationalized in May. On 3 October she evacuated the staff of the Anglo-Iranian Oil Company from Abadan. She returned to Chatham on 18 December,

* For an account of her part in the Corfu Incident, see summary of service of *Saumarez* and *Volage*.

1951, and was refitted at the Palmers' yard on the Tyne during 1952–53.

She was afterwards in the Reserve Fleet, Portsmouth, and on 11 September, 1959, was downgraded to Extended Reserve. Sold to Thomas Ward Ltd. for scrap in March, 1965.

Battle Honours awarded to the *Mauritius* were:

Atlantic	1941
Sicily	1943
Salerno	1943
Mediterranean	1943–44
Anzio	1944
Normandy	1944
Biscay	1944
Norway	1945

H.M.S. LEANDER
Summary of Service

H.M.S. *Leander* was the name-ship of a class of six-inch gun cruisers of 7,270 tons displacement, and was built at Devonport Dockyard, with machinery by Vickers-Armstrongs Limited. She was laid down on 8 September, 1930, launched on 24 September, 1931, and completed on 24 March, 1933.

She served in the Home Fleet until 1937, and on 30 April of that year was recommissioned for service in the New Zealand Division of the Royal Navy. Before leaving for Auckland she represented this force at the Coronation Naval Review on 20 May, 1937.

On the outbreak of the Second World War, the New Zealand cruisers *Leander* and *Achilles* were at sea covering the South Pacific trade routes. In May, 1940 the *Leander*, after escorting the troop convoy US 3 between Fremantle and the Indian Ocean, proceeded to Colombo and joined the East Indies Station. On 20 October, convoy BN 7, which she was escorting, was bombed when south-east of Massawa, without damage. The same night, two Italian destroyers attacked, one of which, the *Francesce Nullo*, was sunk next morning by the destroyer *Kimberley*, another of the escorts. On 29 November, in support of the campaign against Italian Somaliland, the *Leander* bombarded Mogadishu, where her Walrus aircraft also bombed a fish cannery.

On 27 February, while engaged on a search for enemy raiders, the *Leander* intercepted and sank the Italian auxiliary cruiser *Ramb I*, west-south-west of the Maldive Islands.

On 4 March, with the Australian cruiser *Canberra*, the *Leander* intercepted two ships, the Norwegian tanker *Ketty Brovig*, which had been captured by the pocket battleship *Admiral Scheer*, and the German motor vessel *Coburg*, from Massawa. Both vessels were sunk south-east of the Seychelles.

On 23 March, 1941, the *Leander* intercepted the Vichy French steamship *Charles L.D.*, bound for Reunion from Diego Suarez, Madagascar, and sent her into Mauritius under armed guard.

After the German-inspired revolt in Iraq on 4 April by Rashid Ali, the *Leander* was among the ships which escorted troops to Basra, where she arrived, flying the flag of the Commander-in-Chief East Indies, on the 18th. The troops landed unopposed and the Commander-in-Chief left in the *Leander* on the 23rd to return to Colombo.

In May, with the consent of the New Zealand Prime Minister, the *Leander* left for the Mediterranean, arriving at Alexandria on 4 June. Four days later the campaign against Syria began. On the 16th she took part in an action with two Vichy French destroyers off Beirut.

From 18 July, 1941, the *Leander* took part in an operation for the reinforcement of British forces in Cyprus. On the 27th, she left Alexandria to return to New Zealand. The thanks of the Admiralty were conveyed to the New Zealand Navy Board for the generous way in which this ship had been placed at the disposal of other commands, and admiration was expressed of her excellent work on the East Indies and Mediterranean Stations.

In January, 1942, Japan having entered the war, an Anzac Area and Anzac Force was constituted, which the *Leander* joined, under the command of Vice-Admiral H. F. Leary, U.S. Navy. This force covered the eastern and north-eastern approaches to Australia and New Zealand, protecting shipping and supporting the defence of islands in the area, escorting convoys to and from Suva, Noumea and other ports, and the like.

On 13 July, 1943, the *Leander* took part in an action between an Allied task force under Rear-Admiral W. L. Ainsworth, U.S.N., and a Japanese force in the Kula Gulf, between Kolombangara and the mainland of New Georgia. The enemy was practically annihilated. The *Leander* was hit by a torpedo from a submarine and severely damaged. She was out of action for the rest of the war. After being repaired at the U.S. Navy Yard at Boston, Massachusetts, she left there on 27 August, 1945 for Montreal and Rosyth.

From August, 1946 to the end of 1947 the *Leander* served in the 1st Cruiser Squadron, Mediterranean Fleet. She was reduced to reserve in 1948 and scrapped in 1949.

The following Battle Honour was awarded to the *Leander*:

Kula Gulf, 1943

APPENDIX IV

This account of the part Saumarez *played in the sinking of the German battle cruiser* Scharnhorst *was written by an officer who was aboard the destroyer at the time. It originally appeared in* Our Ships at War, *produced by Hawthorn Leslie, builders of the* Saumarez *and many other fighting ships.*

H.M.S. *Saumarez* left Hebburn on 23 June, 1943, for trials and on 4 July joined the Home Fleet at Scapa to 'work up'. During the first week in August the 'work up' was interrupted to escort the Prime Minister to Canada. He crossed the Atlantic in the *Queen Mary* to visit President Roosevelt. *Saumarez* together with *Scourge* steamed at economical speed to the middle of the Atlantic and waited for the *Queen Mary* to overtake them, the idea being that destroyers and cruisers that had escorted the *Queen Mary* from Northern Ireland should hand their escort over to the two 'S' Class destroyers who would then steam at high speed for thirty-six hours until met by destroyers from Canada. As it turned out the visibility at the rendezvous was only a few yards so the *Queen Mary* was not seen, but only heard on the radio. Later course was set for Newfoundland to fuel and thence return to Scapa at twenty knots.

On her return to Scapa *Saumarez* was considered to be sufficiently worked up and several voyages were made escorting convoys to North Russia. As an alternative to this somewhat dreary job, *Saumarez* acted as part of the screen to the Battle fleet patrolling near the convoy in case of attack by enemy surface ships.

On 12 December, 1943, *Saumarez* slipped from her buoy at Scapa on just such another of these operations. The Commander-in-Chief, Home Fleet, Sir Bruce Fraser, sailed in the *Duke of York* with *Jamaica* and a screen of *Savage, Scorpion, Stord, Saumarez,* but after leaving Iceland, instead of patrolling off Bear Island

175

(roughly 120 miles North of North Cape in Norway) as was usual, he went to North Russia, passing within eighty miles of the German bases in Norway. The enemy was not to be drawn and we returned to Iceland to fuel and, incidentally, celebrate Christmas. We knew we should be at sea on the 25th so we had our turkey and parties on the 22nd instead.

Each Christmas the Hun had made a tip and run attack on our convoys to Russia and we were interested to see if he would repeat the performance this year. It was with some excitement that we sailed on the morning of 23 December to cover both an outward bound and homeward bound convoy from Murmansk.

All doubt as to whether the enemy would venture to sea was dispelled at 0300 on the 26th, when a signal was received from the Admiralty telling us that the German battle cruiser *Scharnhorst* was at sea.

At 0830 our cruisers, who were about thirty miles from the convoy, detected the enemy and we knew that if only we could intercept her, now was our chance to destroy the last effective heavy ship left to the enemy. The cruisers did magnificently and, after a few hours of the *Scharnhorst* trying to evade the cruisers and strike for the convoy, she gave up the idea and headed for home. Meanwhile the *Duke of York* and ourselves steamed at our best speed to intercept her; there was a heavy sea running and all depended on how well the ships could take it, whether we should get there in time. They could take it and we did!

At about 1650 in the dark, *Duke of York* opened fire with star-shell and illuminated the *Scharnhorst* about six miles away. A running engagement ensued but the *Scharnhorst*, who had the speed of the *Duke of York*, gradually drew away. The only chance was for the destroyers to reduce her speed with torpedoes. But to do that you have to get within about two miles of the target to have a reasonable chance of hitting her.

An early hit by the *Duke of York* did reduce the speed of the enemy, nevertheless there was a stubborn chase testing the skill and workmanship put into the building of these ships. The speed reached on trials for the designed horse-power gave only about half a knot more than the *Scharnhorst* but *Saumarez* exceeded this speed and in fact steamed for more than an hour at seven revolutions above those obtained on trials. For eleven minutes the guns fired continuously without a jam, the radar functioned faultlessly throughout, this in face of an enemy who was firing three 11-inch guns of his main armament at the ship, which was naturally being thrown around in a drastic manner to avoid being hit. One of these shells, fortunately it didn't explode, passed through the director tower, killing three of the crew and, of course, putting it out of action. It wasn't until a near miss sprayed the ship with fragments and one of these splinters punctured the forced lubrication system that *Saumarez* was checked in her attack.

By then it didn't matter as the ship had fired her torpedoes. One or more hits were obtained and these, together with torpedoes from the rest of the flotilla, brought the *Scharnhorst* to a standstill. The *Duke of York* and cruisers made short work of her. Three hours after the *Duke of York* first illuminated the target, she sank.

Saumarez steamed to Murmansk on one engine and was temporarily repaired by the Russians. On 6 January she left for home and a refit at her builders. A very fine job was made and in a few weeks she was at sea again, fitter than ever and ready to take part in the invasion of Europe.

APPENDIX V

The following account of the Corfu tragedy, as seen through Corfiot eyes, comes from a man who was aged twenty at the time. He kept a diary from the moment the four warships sailed into Corfu Harbour. During the war he served as an interpreter to British Forces, and his account is published just as he wrote it.

22 October, 1946

I see from my window that the two destroyers sailed, by about mid-day towards the Southern Strait—then they returned and headed towards the Northern Strait of Corfu. By about 6.30 pm it was rumoured that the destroyers had been mined while crossing the Northern Strait. A lot of people rushed to the port, only too anxious to learn the news. Later there arrived some wounded British sailors, and some killed, much to the sadness of the population of Corfu. There was also a rumour that the British warships had been shelled and torpedoed from the Albanian Coast.

23 October, 1946

Being myself upset and anxious on these events I mounted my bicycle early in the morning and went to the port at 7.30 am. There I saw anchored H.M.S. *Leander* and H.M.S. *Ocean*. Two destroyers had been tied by their sterns to H.M.S. *Leander*. One of these destroyers had its bow low in the sea (H.M.S. *Saumarez*). Meanwhile H.M.S. *Mauritius* was slowly sailing slightly to the south of the point as if on patrol duty. Soon there arrived from the south a hospital ship. By 8.30 am there came from the south the cruiser H.M.S. *Liverpool*, escorted by a destroyer. They both anchored in the port. I have just learned that the damaged destroyers are H.M.S. *Saumarez* and H.M.S. *Volage*. It is rumoured the estimated number of wounded is thirty, plus six who disappeared

24 October, 1946

Today there took place the funeral processions of ten killed sailors in the mined destroyers. British and Greek sailors and their officers took part. The local people are really sad for the event. Sad. Deeply sad.

This evening I saw in the port a platoon of sailors in file returning from some sort of duty. They were all unshaven and wore no caps. Their uniform looked not clean nor were they pressed—perhaps a sort of fatigue duty uniform. What strikes me most is their gloomy faces—and most rightly so! But should they march with faces down, the proud sailors of the British Navy?

25 October, 1946

A special floating workshop vessel arrived from the south this morning at 8.40 (*Ranpura*) apparently for the purpose of repairing the mined destroyers.

At 4 pm took place the funeral procession of a further two British sailors who died of their wounds. The procession was from the Municipal Hospital morgue to the British Cemetery less than 500 metres away. Both the municipal hospital and British Cemetery were built during the years that the island of Corfu was under British protectorate. It looks as though these two nations are permanently linked because of the sea.

26 October, 1946

At 8.30 am two destroyers and a cruiser set out due south. At 9.30 am there followed H.M.S. *Mauritius* escorted by a destroyer. The following vessels still remain in the port—the two mined destroyers, the hospital ship and the floating workshop.

It is rumoured that a small British vessel equipped with divers is checking the North Strait in the place where the incident took place in order to find out any mines that might have been recently anchored. Certainly, the whole affair was instigated by the Russians!!

Those sailors who had been reported missing were not yet found to this day.

3 November, 1946

The usual procession of Corfu's patron saint, Spyridon, took place today. A lot of pious people followed the procession, while some 2,000 others stood alongside the streets to look at the array. At least half these same people had rushed on 24 October to the British cemetery to honour, to mourn the ten killed British sailors during the funeral. The people of Corfu considered it an affront, this Communist provocation of mining British warships in our waters! No—not only an affront, it was a *crime*—and we all want justice.

INDEX

The ranks of officers and men of the Royal Navy are the latest known to the author.

Admiralty, 8, 10, 28, 66–8, 72, 75, 95, 100, 103, 111, 114–19
Albania, 1, 3, 4, 11, 24, 28, 48, 51, 67, 80, 94, 100, 103, 109–12, 114, 115, 119, 121–3, 126, 128, 130, 132–4, 142, 144, 147, 149–51, 153, 154
Albanian League, 13
Albertz, Captain (German Navy), 129
Aranha, Dr, 127
Argostoli, 10, 22, 24, 25, 66, 109
Attlee, Clement 5, 76, 122

Backa, Albanian Battery Commander, 5, 149
Baldachino, Leading Steward, 82
Bannerman, Torpedo Gunner, 97
Barchetta Rock, 39, 85
Bari, Italy, 135, 139, 140
Beckett, Sir Eric, 141, 150
Bevin, Ernest, 122, 128
Boyd-Carpenter Mr, MP, 151, 153

Cadogan, Sir Alexander, 123
Cape Kefalu, 112
Clarke, Capt A. W., 103, 108
Clinton, HMS, 107
Churchill, Winston, 18, 117, 134
Corfu Channel, 1, 11, 24–9, 46, 55, 67, 85, 96, 99, 109, 111, 115, 128, 132, 133, 138, 141, 147, 148
Cot, M. Pierre, 9, 10, 27, 95, 144–8
Croome, Lieut-Cdr W. P. T., 89, 90–2.

Daily Herald, 135

Davies, Ernest, MP, 150, 151
Daxner, Judge, 135
Denta Point, 79
Dugdale, J., MP, 117

Edge-Partington, Capt Keppel, 23, 37, 106
Edmondson, the Hon John (later Baron Sandford), 37

Fiume, 129
Ford, Engine Room Artificer, 41

Godsal, Capt Walter, 29
Goodman, Stoker Stanley, 71
Griffiths, Engine Room Artificer, 42
Gromyko, Mr, 124, 127
Gueritz, Rear Admiral E. F., 37, 76, 81–3, 97, 101, 105, 118

Hall, "Nobby", 63, 64
Hawthorn Leslie, Wallsend, 109
Hicks Beach, Lieut, 57, 70, 71, 96, 97
Hodges, Petty Officer, 48, 49, 96
Hoxha, Enver, 3, 16, 17, 18, 67, 99, 100, 109, 110, 115, 124, 131, 132, 154

International Court, 8, 9, 27, 94, 127, 133, 134, 139, 140, 141, 149, 152, 153

John, Capt Caspar (Later First Sea Lord), 60, 89

Jones, J. Mervyn, 141

Kapo, Mr, 122–7
Keeton, SPO Cyril, 71
Kinahan, Rear Admiral H.R., 2, 4, 6,
    10, 23, 29, 39, 51, 52, 55, 56, 60,
    75, 91, 97, 111
Kovacik, Lieut-Cdr Karel, 135–40,
    142, 146, 149, 153
Knollys, Lieut-Cdr, Hugh, 34, 38, 99
Knott, P.O. Joseph, 71

Lane, Naval Airman V., 87, 92
Lange, Dr, 126
Lankester, Lieut-Cdr, 39
League of Nations, 116
Leander, H.M.S., 10, 20, 23, 25, 32,
    51, 53, 54–6, 73, 76, 84, 85, 91, 93,
    94, 153
Lewis, Roy, 63
Lie, Trygvie, U.N. Secretary
    General, 109
Limioni Hill, 27, 52
Liverpool, H.M.S., 67, 98

Maine, H.M.S., 85, 87, 99, 102, 106
Maliq Bey, 13, 15
Malta, Island of, 22, 30, 82, 100, 101,
    104, 105, 107, 143
Mauritius, H.M.S., 10, 20, 23, 25, 27,
    30, 32, 39, 51, 60, 61, 66, 75, 76,
    84, 85, 141, 153
Medri Channel, 26, 27, 30, 111, 113,
    128
Mediterranean Fleet, 1, 5, 7, 60
Medzon Board, 26, 100, 111, 124
Meljene, Yugoslav minelayer, 135–8,
    145
Mestre, Cdr, 111, 113
Mitchell, Sick Berth Attendant, 49
Mljet, Yugoslav minelayer, 136–8,
    145
Moullec, Admiral, 95
Murphy, Leading Seaman, 47

Nash, Lieut S. A., 68, 69, 75, 79

Ocean, H.M.S., 27, 60, 61, 84, 92, 96
Operation Retail, 111, 113, 115, 125,
    141, 149

Orion, H.M.S., 1–4, 18, 25–8, 67, 110
O'Riordan, Surgeon-Lieut, 49, 106
Otway-Ruthven, Capt R. K. O.
    25, 53

Padua, Italy, 143
Panikovac Cove, 136, 137, 146, 149
Paul, Commander Reginald, 30,
    52, 55–60, 68–70, 72–5, 77–81,
    85, 94, 95, 107, 142
Phillips, Lieut, 113
Piraeus, Port of Athens, 66, 98
Price, Sub-Lieut H. G., 68–70, 72,
    78

Raider, H.M.S., 60, 84, 86, 89
Ranpura, Fleet-depot ship, 104, 105
Russia, 3, 115, 127, 130

Saranda, 3, 6, 27, 29, 34, 56, 59, 60,
    110, 112, 113, 138, 149
Saumarez, H.M.S., 4, 20, 23, 25, 29,
    30, 32, 33, 38, 39, 43, 45, 50–2,
    54–62, 66, 68–70, 74–7, 79–82,
    84–6, 88–94, 96–109, 112, 113,
    118, 121, 123, 124, 129, 133, 141,
    144, 148, 153, 154
Scharnhorst, 109
Scott, Rear Admiral David, 59, 60,
    79
Selby, Rear Admiral W. H., 29, 30,
    34, 38, 50, 56, 70, 74, 77, 79, 80,
    83, 85, 86, 91, 95, 97, 98, 102,
    105, 118, 142,
Shackleton, Lieut J., 42, 70
Spiller, Engine Room Artificer
    F. W. H., 40, 41
Stalin, Marshal, 16, 17, 126, 131
St Day, H.M.S., 107
Stopford, Captain the Hon Terence,
    35, 37, 103
Swan Hunter, 2
Swift, A.B. George, 78
Superb, H.M.S., 1–4, 18, 25–8, 67,
    110
Seabear, H.M.S., 112
Shawcross, Sir Hartley (Lord Shaw-
    cross), 135, 141, 142, 145
Sibenik, Yugoslavia, 135–8, 140,
    144, 145, 147, 149
Skipjack, H.M.S., 112

Soskice, Sir Frank (Lord Stow Hill), 95, 142, 143, 144, 147
Sylvia, H.M.S., 112
Sworder, Cdr E. R. D., 129

The Times, 110, 111, 117, 118, 120
Tirana, 99, 121, 132
Tito, Marshal, 17, 129–31
Trieste, 129, 131
Truelove, H.M.S., 112
Truman, President H., 119, 120
Tunnicliffe, E. G., 34

Udine, Italy, 143
U.N.O., 100, 116, 117, 119, 121, 122, 126, 127, 133

Valetta, Malta, 19
Vendetta, 15
Volage, 4, 20, 25, 26, 32, 49, 51–3, 55–7, 59, 60, 66, 68, 69, 72–8, 80, 81, 84–6, 88, 91, 93, 94, 96, 102–5, 107–9, 112, 113, 118, 121, 123, 124, 128, 133, 141, 144, 148, 153, 154

Welfare, H.M.S., 112
Wells-Cole, Lieut-Cdr, Peter, 35, 37, 102
Whitford, Cdr Q. P., 112–15
Wilberforce, Lord, 141
Willis, Admiral Sir Algernon, 5, 6, 8, 10, 30, 66, 84, 98, 99, 102–4, 106, 107

X.C.U. (Code name for Corfu Operation), 2, 4, 27

Yugoslavia, 3, 121, 129, 132, 143

Zarb, Petty Officer, 104, 154
Zogu, Ahmed (Later King Zog), 13–16